CLAUSTROPHOBIA

finding your way out

OTHER BOOKS BY ANDREA PERRY

Isn't It About Time? How to stop putting
things off and get on with your life

The Little Book of Procrastination

Andrea Perry taught in Japan before returning to the UK to work in
mental health. She qualified as an integrative psychotherapist, ran a private
practice for twelve years, and is a former Chair of the British Association of
Dramatherapists. Her ground-breaking work on procrastination was covered
extensively in the media, and she provides training, public presentations and
consultancy to student counselling service staff, collaborative family lawyers,
coaches, career and debt counsellors, and human relations staff from the
private and public sector. She is based in London, and is making a garden in
southern France with her husband.

CLAUSTROPHOBIA

finding your way out

Hope and help for people who fear
and avoid confined spaces

ANDREA PERRY

Worth Publishing

www.worthpublishing.com

First published 2008 by Worth Publishing Ltd
9 Charlotte Road, London SW13 9QJ
www.worthpublishing.com

Printed and bound in Great Britain by Biddles, King's Lynn, UK

British Library Cataloguing in Publication Data
A catalogue record for this book is available from the British Library

ISBN   9781903269091

Cover and text design by Anna Murphy
Cover image by Builder Lounge

Acknowledgements

Firstly, I would like to thank all the people who were willing to complete questionnaires about their experiences of claustrophobia, and their strategies for coping with it, either in writing or through interview. I am grateful for their courage and openness, and hope that recognising their voices amongst others with similar experiences will give a sense of solidarity. Thanks to the many other people who told me their tales of claustrophobia in cafés, on trains, in hotels, at work, over meals - I've found there's always a story and a view whenever the subject comes up. I'm grateful to those who passed on my queries to their friends and relatives, and were supportive of the project even when they had not experienced claustrophobia themselves.

I'm grateful to Worth Publishing for taking on this project and being so supportive: for my readers and their invaluable feedback: and Anna Murphy for her wonderful designs, attention to detail, patience and her most welcome sense of humour.

I've been fortunate in receiving assistance from many different sources whilst researching, and would like to thank: the staff at the Upright MRI Centre in London: the staff at the Open MRI unit and press office at the Nuffield Orthopædic Centre: Gill Thomas, hypnotherapist: Ashley Meyer, EFT practitioner: Bronwen Astor, psychoanalyst: Rachel North, author: Nikki Leadbetter of the National Phobics Society: staff at the London Underground Customer Services: Idris Williams of the British Caving Association: Jon

Williams of Passenger Customer Relations, Eurotunnel: Customer Services at Virgin Trains: Customer Services of Otis Lift Company: Inger Beaty-Powall, architect: and Vincent Kirk, of kke Architects, for their time and thoughtfulness.

I'd like to thank my friends, whose love and support has accompanied my own journey out of claustrophobia. Andri White, whose early encouragement meant so much, and who always inspires me with her dynamism: Tsafi Lederman, for sharing my journey, for her belief in the project, and for the glory and abandon of laughing together: Jenny Stacey, for her life-affirming joyfulness and endless encouragement: Tony Lancaster, for his straightforward thinking and generosity: Jane Fisher-Norton for her support on my first trip back on the underground: Bruce Currie, Jo Gaskell, Catherine Pestano, Ann Crump, Geoff Pelham: Evelyn Arnell, Tina Johansson, Bibi Evans, Petra Howard-Wuerz, Jane Eddington, Jean Lancaster, Juliet Bullock, Holly Dwyer, Pittu and Anne Laungani, Brian and Liz Hayward, for their wit, wisdom and constant warmth. They've been with me whilst I was burrowed away writing, and they've welcomed me back out, blinking in the sunlight.

Finally, I'd like to thank my husband and step-children, who have supported me whether I was resisting lifts, having panic attacks in planes, shuttles and cars, regaling them with minute detail of my latest adventure in overcoming claustrophobia, or up to my ears in writing and demanding tea with menaces. Their love, patience, and good humour have been great gifts.

For my parents,
whose love of the natural world
inspired my own:
and for all those imprisoned
by walls or by fear

Contents

Part 1   Get me out of here!   1

1   The inside story of claustrophobia   3

2   The experience of claustrophobia   20

3   How claustrophobia affects our lives   29

4   What causes claustrophobia?   46

Part 2   Is it getting worse?   70

5   The past, present and future of confined space   71

6   Canaries in the coalmine   87
          - claustrophobia and inclusive design

Part 3   Finding your way out   97

7   What helps? An overview   98

8   Self-help strategies   108

9   Confined spaces re-visited   174
          - lifts, MRI scanners, the underground
          and other forms of transport

(continues ...)

10 Finding support through therapy **200**

11 Beyond claustrophobia **245**

Appendix A Creating a hierarchy of goals **249**

Appendix B Post-traumatic stress disorder **252**

Appendix C Recommendations for the design of spaces that hold humans **254**

Resources **256**

References **259**

Addendum **262**

Part 1

Get me out of here!

2   Claustrophobia

Chapter I

The inside story of claustrophobia

Claustrophobia is the fear of confined spaces, a fear I had for several years. It may affect up to ten percent of the population, which means potentially six million people in the UK could have the experience at some point in their lives. It's a life-limiting anxiety, creating difficulties with travel, with continuing work or changing jobs, going on holiday, taking lifts, or even benefiting from advances in medical technology. Claustrophobia is an extremely unpleasant experience that can arrive out of the blue when we least expect it, to anyone, of any age, and it can get worse if we continue to avoid the confined spaces we find so difficult.

But our anxiety may, in part, be an entirely rational response to the discomforts and dangers of some confined spaces. I've come to think that within claustrophobia lies a profoundly human rejection of the alienation and dangers that technical advances have the potential to create. So if we can overcome the *irrational* aspects of our claustrophobia, we will be in a better position to make the *rational* case for the development of a safer, more human-centred environment, as technology and a shifting social climate change the way we live.

This book is written to help people who experience claustrophobia go back to the confined spaces they - and I - have avoided. It's entitled - *Claustrophobia: Finding Your Way Out*, because as someone who's known the phobia from the inside, I believe there's no one single technique, method, therapeutic process or even magic wand that works for everyone, because we're all different, with different needs and experiences.

In this book, you'll find a huge range of possibilities to try out and experiment with, noticing the advantages and disadvantages, until you find what is right for you. Many people have contributed their experiences of claustrophobia, as well as their strategies for overcoming it. Some people were kind enough to send their contributions, and in other cases we met up and talked through thoughts and experiences. Some people wanted me to take notes, since writing about their anxiety was too stressful. I admire their courage in being willing to have the conversation.

Others became so anxious talking about claustrophobic experiences that they had to stop part-way, or indeed, stop completely. For some this was a self-protective and sensible thing to do, rather than staying in a situation in which they felt they might be overwhelmed. An essential skill we all need to develop is knowing when it would be better to avoid or remove ourselves from an anxiety-producing situation (reducing the possibility of re-traumatisation by being overwhelmed), and when there might be value in having a go and carrying on when we feel anxious, building our tolerance of anxiety, and developing a sense of mastery.

Whichever path we take, when we feel claustrophobic anxiety, we can remind ourselves that we are not passive; there is always something we can do. We are in control of our choices, and we can learn from the results of any choices we make.

Were all the discussions and contributions harrowing? Certainly not! On many occasions there was also a lot of laughter and humour: not only because it was a great way to release some of the tension caused by talking and thinking about claustrophobia, but also because occasionally there are some genuinely funny things that happen in avoiding or being caught in small spaces.

Many of us have experienced shame about having claustrophobic anxieties - we're adults, aren't we? Shouldn't we be able to cope? So being able to see the funny side of the situations we've got into is a great antidote; the life-limiting ice of shame doesn't survive long in the shared understanding and warmth of gentle - or even uproarious! - laughter.

Real, earthy laughter does everything for us that a phobia can't. It's relaxing. It releases tensions. It gives us a great surge of 'feel-good' hormones. It restores a sense of proportion and perspective, and it gives us enough strength and confidence to go on, to pick ourselves up (again) and to take the next courage-building step. To share humour is to shake off phobias' clammy grip, to have hope again. To laugh is to feel free. And feeling free is the opposite of feeling trapped, whether we're still in the small space or not.

This book may also help people who don't experience claustrophobia, but who'd like a deeper insight into what it is like, and perhaps be moved to view the world through a slightly different lens. Some may want ideas to help people they care about. Others may be involved with creating buildings, spaces, products or services, and if so, I hope you'll allow your new awareness to influence your approach to design.

About reading Claustrophobia ...
If you're someone who experiences claustrophobia, please consider these questions before reading any further:

Will reading about other people's experiences of claustrophobia help you by *reducing* your sense of isolation about feeling claustrophobic?

> Will reading about other people's experiences help
> you *increase your tolerance* of thinking about claustrophobic
> experiences, thus moving you towards your goal of
> managing the anxiety of the real situation?

or -

> Will reading about other people's experiences *increase*
> your anxiety and maybe even give you new things to be
> anxious about?

If you feel that reading other people's experiences will make you feel worse, please don't read further at this point. Please concentrate instead on the section of this book that offers you strategies for reducing anxiety and for overcoming claustrophobia. This section starts on p. 97.

On the other hand, if you want to continue reading, on pages 16-19 you'll find three quick and simple techniques to turn to if the going gets tough. Any or all of these techniques may also help you to go into or through the small and confined spaces you and I have both avoided.

If those strategies work for you, you might one day come back to this section of the book and think, quite calmly, *"Oh yes - I used to feel like that. And I don't now"*. That is my sincere wish and hope for you. The choice is yours.

It's only fair to share my own experiences with you first. I've had a vague sense of being claustrophobic as long as I can remember. I've been through a period where the full-blown terror of being trapped in an enclosed space restricted practically all my movement, especially travel, as I avoided more and more possibilities of being confined. That's not how things are now. I've gradually worked my way back through almost everything I came to avoid. It's still a work in progress, but I look back with compassion and pride, and ahead with confidence and hope.

Until quite recently I couldn't travel alone in lifts, or enter them if they were very crowded. I couldn't travel by tube. I wouldn't go in the back seat of a two-door car. I really hated tunnels, especially long ones with curves. I couldn't go and look around an ancient monument or castle or cathedral if there might be a spiral staircase or narrow passages without windows.

I've been escorted through the backs of hotels to find stairs that newly appointed staff didn't even know existed, and led to my room through baffling mazes of corridors that would defeat even a quick-witted rat. I couldn't put on a motorcycling helmet or contemplate deep-sea diving. I hated putting my head under water. I couldn't use loos that were electronically controlled (which meant keeping legs crossed on long train journeys) and as soon as I got into a hotel room with electronic locks I checked that the door would open easily from the inside. And if you had invited me to come and see you, and you gave me directions such as, *take the tube to my office in the City and then the lift to the seventeenth floor* - I'd have asked to meet you elsewhere.

And use a car-wash? I don't think so. MRI scanner - only if my life had been severely threatened, and even then ... Flotation tank? Voluntarily? Pass. The London Eye? Sealed in a glass bubble suspended high above the water ... hmm, let me think about it ...

And I felt ashamed to be so scared. The shame was associated with feeling helpless, or like a child, incapable of functioning independently. Having to ask for special consideration - *I need to go in the front of the car, we can't go through the Dartford Tunnel (so we get stuck forever in traffic jams taking the long way round), would you stand outside the loo on the boat as I can't lock the door, will you come down in the lift to meet me from your tenth-floor flat*. Not wanting to call it a disability, but feeling disabled. And thus further ashamed, because people who are genuinely disabled have no choice. And we who experience claustrophobia look very much as if we have a choice. And we do. But it so often doesn't feel like that, when all we can see is terror.

I'm a psychotherapist, I knew all the right theories, and yet despite my best efforts, fear gripped me by the throat, and all my instincts were to escape, escape, escape. I felt weak, immature, unprofessional. And very stuck. I'd even written books about procrastination, which is another kind of stuck, and worked with many, many people to find the kind of techniques that could get their lives moving again. And we celebrated together when those techniques worked, time and time again, even for people who had been at the end of their tether and felt hopeless. But somehow I kept avoiding confined spaces, justifying myself by thinking I was too busy, too tired, too … you get the picture. I was avoiding with a capital A, and it wasn't helping.

Has reading this made you feel anxious? Notice your breathing, and if you are experiencing physical tension. If simply reading these words, envisioning these situations has already caused you stress, you're probably also someone who experiences or has experienced claustrophobia quite badly.

You don't need to stay with this book or feel trapped. You can dip in and out, as I suggested earlier (p. 6). Take a few deep breaths, maybe walk around the block, ask someone to give you a hug, stroke the cat or go and do a Sudoku. Anything that will calm you, release stress, enable you to support your emotional self to feel more calm and grounded, and your rational self to continue to think and reflect.

Of course, if you prefer, you can carry on reading, knowing that words on a page are not going to trap you, and as a way of improving your tolerance of anxiety, getting used to the imagery.

You make the choices, and notice how it feels to know you have that control. And please recognise that by even contemplating reading a book on claustrophobia, you've begun to challenge the problem, which is genuine progress. Take your time, do it bit by bit, and please don't traumatise yourself in the process.

It wasn't always been as bad for me as I've described above. When I was younger I travelled not only all over London by underground, but even commuted daily in Tokyo for three years. Of course sometimes the trains stopped in tunnels between stations for a while (though I don't recall the very long delays that seem to occur now) and I do remember the early tentacles of fear beginning to creep up from my stomach. But I coped. In the early '80's, some London tube-trains had slatted wooden floors and since in those days smoking was permitted on the tube (unimaginable now!), sometimes cigarette butts, their tips lightly glowing, would lodge and even vaguely smoulder between the slatts. So the situation was far from super-safe, even before potential threats from would-be terrorists. Like most people probably, I didn't like those experiences, but the feelings of claustrophobia were somehow manageable.

And indeed, I've been trapped - as a child, locked in a cellar as a misguided "joke" by an elderly relative: and underwater, being pulled out to sea by a powerful current. I would have been lost if not for my quick-witted father. But neither of these events led me to avoid the ordinary small spaces we all encounter on a daily basis.

So what changed? Why should I become so much more claustrophobic now than I was then? Why did so many situations seem problematic? Was it 'simply' getting older and needing to be more in control, or seeing more news and films portraying people being trapped in situations I'd never thought of? Or was it electronically controlled modern life creating more and more claustrophobia-inducing circumstances?

For me there was something of a 'tipping point' going on holiday with my partner and his thirteen year-old son. We had planned to drive down to the South of France, and were very excited. We left Central London around lunch-time, thinking to arrive at the Channel Tunnel to put the car on the train mid-afternoon, and to then take it in turns to drive down through France during the night. I'd been on coaches through the Tunnel twice before, not enjoying either experience, but somehow coping (consuming huge quantities of food helped, as I recall, including making sure that I got my fair share of Doritos). So whilst I wasn't particularly looking forward to this part of the journey, I wasn't pre-occupied with anxiety about it either.

Trying to get out of London was a nightmare. There were huge road-blocks and delays, and our long journey ground to an early halt beside Tower Bridge. We sat there for such a long time that in retrospect it would have been better to have turned round and found another way, or even gone the next day. But we were so keen to go, and we kept making a little progress here and there, so we stuck at it. Outside London eventually, and out into Kent, I fell asleep, exhausted, and it was only as we were driving down the entry tunnel beside the train that I woke up, with a start.

All I could see was wall and metal. Above us, to the side, the walls were literally closing in as the car entered and drove down the length of the train towards a steel barrier. Windows only at floor level. No way out (I didn't see the passenger corridor door at the side). Surrounded. Completely, utterly, totally trapped. A huge fire-ball of terror ripped upwards from my belly through my diaphragm into my chest.

Still three-quarters asleep, I screamed frantically. I tried to open the door to get out, just as I have leapt out of alien beds trying to find non-existent doors in unfamiliar walls, waking in darkness in terror of being buried alive. But even as my partner turned towards me in alarm, he was bringing the car to a standstill, stuck in the row of boarding cars, and the metal grid was beginning to come down behind the vehicle behind us. I immediately leapt out of our car into the "compartment" (to me a cage within a cage within a cage) in a state of total panic and agitation, desperate to get off the train. But it was really too late. We were sealed in and the train was about to start.

I collapsed back in my seat in floods of tears, filled with a sense of utter doom and dread. My partner tried to soothe me by stroking my arm, which temporarily pulled me out of my hysteria. I felt another, smaller hand on my shoulder, as his son joined in from the backseat. I hadn't forgotten him, but my ability to be an adult had completely disappeared. I swore, cried, screamed and hyperventilated. Over the next thirty minutes, which felt like thirty hours, I gained a degree of control. I tried, for the boy's sake, to rise above my panic, but it returned time after time throughout the journey, and he definitely saw me at my disintegrated worst.

During the journey we ate and drank everything we had in the car, and we played a family pencil-and-paper game called Squares. Normally a really good score in this game is in the high 70's; on a rare occasion, someone scrapes through to the early 80's (out of 100). Deep beneath the Channel, in one epic sweep of the board, I managed a score of 89. I presume all my synapses were firing, charged up as I was with adrenaline with nowhere else to go.

Both the lads wanted to move and explore. All that eating and drinking had had its effect, and they naturally wanted to go off down the corridor which connects each two-car section of the train to find a loo. But I couldn't let them go (in full panic mode, I was more than a little controlling). So that little battle took up a few more minutes, and took me up and down the roller-coaster of terror once again. Sometime in the journey, one of us saw a sign somewhere that seemed to suggest that there was help available at the Terminal for people who experienced claustrophobia. Whilst we couldn't imagine what help this could be - short of a ticket for a boat-trip or a knock-out thump to the back of the head - we logged the information for the return trip.

Once we left the tunnel, I breathed for what felt like the first time in weeks. It was a black and gorgeous night. The sky was clear and still, and a vast moon hung like a golden pumpkin over Calais. I swore at the tunnel, whoever invented this inhumane method of transport, and the whole ghastly experience. And then I heard a small, anxious response from the back-seat. *"But the tunnel isn't bad in itself.   It's you who has the problem, isn't it?"*

I stopped mid-flow. I was suddenly called back to the reality of the thirty year gap between me and this wonderful boy, to my responsibilities as an adult to separate feeling from fact, to not skew his view of the world in an unhelpful direction through my own anxiety. I took a huge breath, bigger than all my terror, bigger than all my imaginings.

"Yes," I said. *"You're right. The tunnel ... is just a tunnel.*
It's me that doesn't like it"

No more was said for quite a while, as we drove on into France. I felt ashamed, helpless, anxious still, and, overwhelmingly, exhausted, but just very very faintly good about having managed to retrieve some grain of adult sensibility and grounding in order to respond to his question.

We had a great few days, exploring Provence, cycling, eating, playing. But for me, lurking in the background like a bad dream that won't leave you even in the broad light of day was the knowledge that the journey would have to be repeated on the way back. I tried hard to push this thought away by reminding myself that it was probably best to get back on the horse after a fall, and anyway, the promised help at the terminal might really be of benefit.

The clocks went back that weekend, but we managed to somehow put ours forward instead. So on arrival at Calais we had plenty of time to look around for the promised assistance. We were sent from desk to desk, but no-one seemed to know who could help. Eventually we came across a young, good-looking, very long and very languid Frenchman, who, on being asked what assistance was available to people who suffered claustrophobia, was moved to uncurl himself. He leant forward over the desk. *"Of course"*, he said, " *I can 'elp"*.

He seemed quite animated by the prospect. My hopes were high. He looked me in the eye with the hauteur of professional confidence.

" What I can say to you, Madame, is - zere is no need to be claustrophobic!".

He lay back in his chair and folded his arms behind his head with the pleased look of a job well done. We were speechless.

We got home. I've completely blanked out the return trip. What I do remember is my partner reassuring me that Channel Tunnel trains never get stuck in the tunnel. What I also remember is being told the following evening that a colleague had been on the train behind ours, and that his train had been stuck in the tunnel for two hours. And that *"After an hour, Alan said that even he began to get a bit anxious"*.

I realised that Alan and I were made of completely different stuff. I wished I could be more like him.

So from then on, I met a wall of panic every time I tried to use the underground (I gave up a few months later), or if I got on a train without open-able windows, taxis, planes (once famously declaring in the middle of a heavy-duty bout of turbulence that I was going to get off the plane - and meaning it), or if I had to face travelling in a lift. The day I realised I would soon be left with no transport at all was the day I realised I had to get a grip.

I was running a workshop, in Edinburgh, on overcoming procrastination. Trainers in the afternoon session were leading an exercise, based on a strategy from my first book, in which we envisaged ourselves taking the first step towards something we'd been putting off, and shared it with a partner. The first thing that came to my mind was claustrophobia. I realised, yet again, that if my work on overcoming procrastination had real validity, it had to work in all kinds of circumstances - including claustrophobia: I really couldn't keep on putting it off. Here was the next challenge for expanding my life, tipped right into my lap by my unconscious. I had to laugh, at having effectively backed myself into my own corner, but I started to feel anxious even at the thought of getting started.

But having made that decision, it has seemed natural to start researching and writing and communicating with people for whom claustrophobia was still a problem, those who had overcome their fears, people for whom it had never been an issue. I love hearing other peoples' stories, and writing about the common ground we find. As you'll find on p. 171, identifying what we love and doing more of it can be a key to overcoming claustrophobia, and it's one of the many strategies that have worked for me. I believed that communicating about claustrophobia to anyone and everyone would reduce its power in my life. I wanted my independence back, not to be cramped and constricted and limited by fears and anxieties.

And that's what's happened. I've been alone and happy in lifts, revolving doors, taxis, buses, trains, cars, loos with any old kind of lock, tunnels and the underground. By the time you read this I'll have been on Eurostar. And through a car-wash. I'm getting there.

So I've written this book for several reasons. Partly to overcome my own fear, in the belief that getting to know the 'enemy' was the best way to defeat it. I wanted to share that journey publicly, so that people who felt shame about their own phobia might know they were not alone; in a way, to bring claustrophobia out into the open. I wrote it in order to learn from other people, and to pass on that learning: to find, and then to share, hope. Hope based in real, positive progress, my own and other peoples', brought about by finding ways to go back to the small, confined spaces that held so much terror for us.

And finally, I've written this book to say to architects, designers, planners, engineers and builders who make our physical world, when you design or create a small space that is intended to hold humans, be it in housing, transport, medical equipment - include a consideration of claustrophobia in your thinking.

If you did, I believe that design standards would improve for all, not only for those of us who experience claustrophobia. We need to recognise that a possible consequence of doing what we do, just because we technically can, is the creation of an electronically controlled environment in which human needs for freedom and relationship are increasingly marginalised. Once we have worked through the irrational aspects of our fears, those of us who experience claustrophobia can use our sensitivity to the built environment, and our imagination, to contribute to the development of a safer, less stressful world for everyone.

So I want buildings that are light and open. I want fresh air to circulate. I want exits easily available and clearly marked. I want windows and doors that can be opened by passengers on trains and buses and in cars, even if all these things mean we travel a little slower. I want real keys in cars and in hotel doors. I want long mirrors in every lift, and alternative stairs that are carpeted and comfortable, not made of rough brick and cement. I want train drivers and pilots to speak to passengers and keep us informed, not leave us in unnecessarily anxiety-provoking silence. I want people to have emotional access to buildings, as well as physical access. And if we get stuck, I want to know we can be reached.

I wish you a safe journey as you find your way out of claustrophobia, and a joyful return to your rightful capacity to go anywhere and do what you want to do, regardless of the size or nature of the spaces in which you find yourself.

THREE QUICK TECHNIQUES FOR (RE)ESTABLISHING A SENSE OF SAFETY

Before you start reading the book, you might like to look through these three suggestions and work out which works best for you. Then, if reading the book makes you feel anxious, you can take time out and use one or more of the techniques to stabilise yourself again.

I Establishing a 'secure base' or safe place

Where do you feel safe? Where do you feel safest? For some people, there's no place like home: their garden: the sofa: their bed. For others, it's somewhere peaceful in the natural environment - a favourite beauty spot, a hill with a view, a beach. Others mention more public places, where there is buzz, people, music, lights and life. And many of us think of a certain person or people as our 'secure base', regardless of location - with my best friend - with my partner - my family - or with an animal we love.

Wherever or whoever constitutes your 'safe place', I'd encourage you to replenish yourself there as often as you need to, and then some more. If you're going to deal with the anxieties of claustrophobia, first build a strong sense that you can go back to your secure base either literally, or in your mind, as and when you want to.

When you're in that place, look around. Really study it in detail. Appreciate its contours, its textures, its colours, its feel, warmth, sounds and smells. Close your eyes when you're there and breathe it in. Allow yourself to feel how safe and relaxed you are. And let your internal image of your safe place become as vivid as the reality.

Sometimes people like to 'anchor' the sense of safety and security in their bodies, to permit easier access at a later date. A simple way of doing this is to find a tiny physical gesture that you can learn to associate with that rich, warm feeling. It could be gently holding your own index finger, thinking about your safe place. It could be gently stroking your arm, thinking how good being in that place makes you feel. It could be as simple as remembering to relax your shoulders, and connecting that release of tension to the marvellous reassurance your safe place brings you. Whatever you decide, strengthen your positive associations to that simple gesture, and practice it when you're relaxed as much as when you're tense.

2 Running to your safe place

Once you've established a firm sense of your safe place, you can draw on the security you experience there to support you. If you begin to feel anxious, at any time including when you are reading this book, you can run there in your imagination. Picture yourself running down the roads on the way back, up or down any steps, round any corners, along any paths, the last bit of the journey, and you're there. Breath in that deep sense of security and safety.

Peter Levine's book *Healing Trauma* (Sounds True, 2005) is full of interesting ways to 'restore the wisdom of your body' after trauma of some kind. He suggests techniques for re-establishing a sense of our ability to be active if we have experienced a situation where escape was thwarted (for example if we were stuck in a large crowd, in a lift, a train, or in any of the situations listed on p. 22). The kind of immobility we may have felt can really add to the fear of being stuck again. Putting a 'memory' of running to safety in our muscles provides an alternative image for the brain to access.

Sit in a comfortable chair, with pillows underneath your feet; close your eyes and imagine you're being chased by a gorilla (preferably a large cartoon one). Feel the strength in your legs. Start making running movements with your legs, and run from wherever you are in your mind's eye as above, all the way to your safe place. If you're a wheelchair user, make the movements with your arms, without actual contact with your chair, racing down that road in your mind's eye all the way back.

Imagine yourself safely back in your secure base, making whatever gestures come to mind at the gorilla, who wanders off to hunt for a banana. Notice your breathing and heartbeat. Allow yourself to shake a bit if you need to. Say *"I did it. I can run. I can take care of myself"*. And feel the power of your warmed-up muscles. You could also visualise racing away from a confined space (instead of the gorilla), just to 'remind' your legs and arms that they have this power.

3 Circles of support

The trauma specialist Felicity de Zulueta* uses 'bubblegrams' to describe the support systems the people we are attached to create around us. To create your own bubblegram, imagine or draw a quick circle in the middle of a piece of paper, and write your name in it.

Then, around you, draw circles for each of the closest people in your life, people (and animals) with whom you have a mutually caring relationship. Put each person's name in a separate 'bubble'. Around this circle, draw or imagine another ring of bubbles containing the names of other people in your life: family members, other friends, colleagues, a counsellor, a teacher, anyone who has every supported you, whether they are still with you now or not.

This is your security system. You can access support when you want to. If these people are not actually present when you're in need, you can call them or imagine their faces, and have conversations with them in your mind. You can picture these people alongside you as you read this book, or if you are experimenting with going into enclosed spaces, or afterwards. Appreciate the sense of support these people provide.

If you're enjoying this process in your mind's eye, you might also like to imagine a further ring of all the people who would help you and wish you well if they heard you were in need - emergency services, charities, kind and thoughtful citizens of every nationality, entrepreneurs and singers known for their generosity ... the world is full of supportive people.

Relish your sense of connection. You are not alone. And of course the more secure and connected any of us feel, the more likely we are to be able to provide warmth and assistance to others.

* Talking Matters Conference, Hatfield, October 2007.

Chapter 2

The experience of claustrophobia

Claustrophobia is more than the powerful sense of *"I've got to get out"* of a confined space. As shorthand, though, *"I'm claustrophobic"* is probably more effective at creating gangways and getting support than lengthier explanations! It's the voice of our extreme anxiety, our panic, driving us to escape from a situation that we feel will overwhelm or is overwhelming our ability to cope, physically, mentally or emotionally. Our *'fight or flight'* reaction has been triggered, by the stimulus of actual or perceived restricted movement or reduced air-flow. We do everything we can to 'fly'.

Some people have been traumatised by being trapped in genuinely life-threatening situations. Others experience profound anxiety for the first time in a situation where logically, they are not physically endangered. Our problems as people who experience claustrophobia develop when we *generalise* from either experience to other situations that somehow remind us of those terrible feelings, but which hold very little risk of danger, or none at all.

Our generalisation can make us over-estimate threats, mis-read a situation, but still experience the powerful urge to escape. It's hard for our primitive survival systems to discriminate between what is really happening and what we believe or imagine is or will be happening. We don't do this consciously. No-one plans to experience panic. But subsequently, we may keep the fear in place in part by what we tell ourselves, continuing to link the experience of fear with the image of a confined space, and by avoiding finding out if our fears are valid.

Fear of being trapped in many confined spaces has a basis in reality (*see* p. 63, *Is claustrophobia completely irrational?*). The *phobic* element of claustrophobia is the reluctance to ever again feel those intense and extreme feelings which we experienced in a small or enclosed space, or have come to associate with those places. Claustrophobia is the persistent avoidance of the situations and triggers which set off our fear, or the potential that we might feel fear. If claustrophobia develops, if we continue to avoid, then we may come to shy away from even looking at or thinking about the places and spaces that cause us anxiety, because the feelings are so uncomfortable when we do so. Deep down we know that the *intensity* of this aspect of our fear is irrational.

What kind of places do we avoid?

The list of confined spaces you'll find below has been collected from all the people I've met and heard from who have experienced claustrophobia. *Every item on the list has been mentioned by more than one person.*

Not everyone will find all of these situations difficult. Many of us will find some of them harder than others. How hard we find any particular situation may vary over time. What is hard today may not have been that bad yesterday, or indeed, may be much easier tomorrow.

If you notice yourself getting at all anxious when you read the list, see if it's possible to detect which items are more (or less) tense-making than others. What is the difference between them? Learning to differentiate will be a great starting point for developing your ability to cope with any or all of them (*see* p. 27).

On this list I haven't included other kinds of situations which might be described as 'emotionally claustrophobic'. For the moment,

I want to stay with the anxieties caused by small or restricted space. But you'll find more about 'emotional claustrophobia' on page 61.

People experience claustrophobia in ...

AEROPLANES, HELICOPTERS
ANYTHING THAT HOLDS OR RESTRICTS movement of the head
ANY SMALL, DARK PLACE
ATTICS

BACK SEAT of a three-door car
BEING TOTALLY UNDER WATER, or simply having one's
        head under water
BOATS with no open deck to walk on, hovercraft
BUSES with automatic closing doors

CABLE CARS
CANAL BOATS ·
CARS - especially those with electronic battery operated keys,
        with central locking systems: cars with no manually
        operated windows: the back seat of two-door cars, or
        with 'kiddie locks': with heavily tinted windows
CAR-PARKS, multi-storey - especially underground with several levels
CAR-WASHES - especially four-sided, electronically closing ones
CAVES
CELLARS
CHANGING ROOMS in shops
CINEMAS - especially sitting in the middle of a row
CLOTHES that only open down the back
COACHES, mini-buses, people carriers - especially in back seats or
        away from windows
CORRIDORS - especially long ones with no windows or Exit signs

CRASH HELMETS or anything that goes over or covers the face
CROWDED PUBLIC PLACES - shop sales, Christmas shopping streets...
CUPBOARDS UNDER STAIRS
DENTAL SURGERIES - especially when the chair is tipped right back
     - especially when a plaster mould is fixed between the teeth, or
     previously, when a mask was used to administer gas
ELECTRONICALLY OPERATED "AIR-LOCK"- STYLE SECURITY
     ENTRANCES
FILMS * picturing scenes of entrapment of all kinds - especially viewed
     in dark cinemas
FIREWORK DISPLAYS with crowds
FUN FAIR "RIDES", especially the ghost train: the London Eye
HISTORIC BUILDINGS or sites of antiquity - especially where there are
     - or might be - unexpected small spaces or narrow passageways
     with limited exits, and where a guide is needed eg the Pyramids
HOTEL ROOMS with electronic doors and sealed, double-glazed
     windows
JURY SERVICE - having to stay in the court and then being locked in a
     room with strangers
LIFTS - especially if they're very small, dark or have no mirror: if they
     are crowded with people: or, conversely, if there is no-one else in
     the lift
LOOS - especially with no gaps at the top of the door or walls:
     especially with heavy doors and deadlocks: loos on planes:
     electronically operated loos on trains or in the street
MASKS
MINES

* This is a bit of an exception, but because it depicts people struggling in small spaces,
  and was mentioned by many people, it seems natural to include it on this list rather
  than in the section on emotional claustrophobia (see p. 61). There is, however,
  discussion of it in Part 3, What helps? p. 158

MOTORCYCLE HELMETS
MRI SCANNERS

PARADES
PARTIES
PEOPLE so close you have to breathe in their out-breath

OVERTAKING on motorways or being surrounded by large high-sided
    lorries

PRISON or being arrested: being handcuffed or put in a police van

REVOLVING DOORS

SCUBA-DIVING
SLEEPING WITH HEAVY OR 'TUCKED IN' BEDDING
STAIRCASES - if they are enclosed, for example on a ship: spiral
        staircases in castles or towers: stairwells provided as an
        alternative to lifts, often bleak areas, made of rough concrete and
        no windows
STRETCH LIMOS
SUBMARINES
SUBWAYS
SWIPE-CARD controlled environments

TAXIS with automatically locking doors
TELEPHONE BOXES (old style)
THEATRES - especially sitting in the middle of a row - especially plays
        with very few characters or movement
THICK CARPETS, sand, mud, or glass which restrict wheelchair mobility
TIGHT OR HEAVY CLOTHES
TRAFFIC JAMS
TRAINS - especially those with automatic closing doors, no open-able
        windows, for example Virgin tilting trains, electronically operated loos
        and - especially Eurostar (a train in a tunnel under the sea ... ruled
        out completely (though with regret) - by many, many contributors)

TUBE TRAINS - especially deep underground ones, especially at
    rush-hour, especially when they stop between stations without
    explanation from the driver, especially in summer
TUNNELS - especially long ones, or ones through which traffic either
    drives very fast or is stuck.
WALK-IN FRIDGES, cold rooms

This is a very wide-ranging list, covering many aspects of day-
to-day life. Some people reading it may be surprised. They may
have thought that claustrophobia was limited to lifts, tube trains
and aeroplanes. Once you understand that all kinds of small and
confined spaces can trigger claustrophobia, for some people, it's
easy to notice how readily anxiety-producing situations crop up in
day-to-day living. It's also interesting – and perhaps concerning
- to see how many of these situations have been created by new
technologies (a subject we'll return to later in Chapters 5 and 6).

So if you experience claustrophobia, recognise and celebrate
your courage in getting on with life, however you have dealt
with your anxieties up to now (and yes, that might have included
avoidance), and how much resilience you've already developed.
And the list may help those who don't experience claustrophobia,
but who know or want to help someone who does, to empathise that
bit more and appreciate how limiting this anxiety can be.

There is no need to feel isolated

Every single item on this list has been identified as 'claustrophobic'
by more than one person in my research. So if you experience
claustrophobia in any or all of these situations, *you are not alone*;
other people do too

And it's likely that if there is yet another situation you've experienced, but that isn't on the list, then someone else will have found it claustrophobic as well – we just haven't asked them yet!*

In fact estimates of the number of people who experience claustrophobia vary between five and fifteen percent of the population - that is a lot of people. (These figures are taken from research on 'refusal rates' from MRI scanning procedures. It is assumed that people referred for MRI scans represent a fair cross-section of the population). So if you experience claustrophobia, you are neither weird nor crazy. You're part of a large group of humans, experiencing a very human response.

Our anxieties and fears are on a continuum of possible responses, like most other reactions. In this case, the continuum runs from -

Very strong anxiety response ------- to ------ No anxiety response

- when presented with a confined space or situation. Wherever you are currently on the continuum, this book will give you a wide choice of strategies all geared towards helping you move in the direction of less anxiety about being confined.

Can looking at this list help you overcome your claustrophobia? It could be a start. Sometimes we become so anxious that we don't even want to think about the situations that cause or have caused our anxiety. Please recognise that you have already taken a huge step forward by simply picking up this book, reading the list, thinking about the situations. Give yourself a real pat on the back, or tangible reward (cups of tea do wonders, in my experience ...).

If you did notice that you felt a little anxious simply looking

* Let me know, and I'll find out - openspace@worthpublishing.demon.co.uk

at the list, then please remind yourself of the choices on p. 8. When we feel anxious, it can seem as if things will just 'happen to us'; as if we are no longer in control. The more we practise exploring and experimenting with what helps, especially when the anxiety is a low level, the more confidence we can build in our ability to make choices, good choices, when the level is higher.

You may be coping better than you realised
Perhaps the list can help you realise how much resilience and creativity you've already used in dealing with some of these situations, despite your anxieties. You've come this far, you've decided to read a book to help yourself go further, so you really are well on your way. Look back at this list again, some time in the future. You'll be able to notice how your responses vary over time, as your range of strategies and tolerance develop, and as you find increasingly effective ways of coping.

Use the list to create a series of challenges or goals (see Appendix A). You can work through them systematically, building confidence in your ability to cope. You could do this alone, with a buddy (*see* p. 143), or with a professional (see p. 200). It's logical to have a go at something least anxiety-provoking first, and you'll find many strategies in Part 3 to help you. On the other hand, circumstances and how you feel at any given time may surprise you, and you may find yourself mixing up the order. Re-visiting the list will remind you of progress you're making or have made, or help keep your intention to do so in your awareness.

Looking for differences
What makes any one item on the list harder or easier than any other, for you? (The clearer you can be about the difference, the better, enabling you to target what you might like to work on).

> What are you *doing* in the easiest-to-manage situation, to help yourself? Could you do more of that?
>
> Are you doing the same thing in the harder-to-manage situation?
>
> If not, what would be the first step in that direction? What would help you take it?
>
> What are you *thinking* in the easier-to-manage situation, and what are you telling yourself in the harder-to-manage situation?
>
> Does thinking in these two situations differ? What helps you most? What different thoughts would help even more?

Recognising that our experience of claustrophobia varies from situation to situation can help challenge the 'all-or-nothing' thinking of phobia. If we remind ourselves, "*Sometimes I experience claustrophobia a bit, sometimes a lot, and sometimes I don't at all*", we can move away from the self-definition -"*I'm claustrophobic*", which can become an always-and-forever self-concept - towards a description of how we respond under particular circumstances. Noting the differences in how we cope can also remind us of our strengths, resourcefulness and creativity, and help highlight what we want to develop.

For example, you may notice that "*I can manage lifts fine when I'm with people I know, but I find them harder when I'm with strangers or alone*". This tells you that the strengths you might want to build include communicating your needs to strangers (p. 190) and/or developing your ability to talk to yourself in constructive ways (*see* p. 138). These are skills that you can develop in all kinds of situations, not only when you are feeling claustrophobic.

Chapter 3

How claustrophobia affects our lives

I Our physical experience

Below are the kinds of physical symptoms people who experience claustrophobia have noticed. We've had these experiences either in a confined space, or if the claustrophobia has become intense, at the sight or thought of a confined space:

Racing or pounding heart/palpitations
Breathing quickly
Tightening in the chest, breathlessness, gasping
Dizziness, pressure on the head
Pulse in the pit of the stomach
Being hyper-alert, agitation - inability to sit still
Dry mouth, diarrhoea, stomach cramps and surges
Feeling sick, queasy
Sweating, feeling very hot or very cold
Huge tension - or - frozen, unable to move

It's important to know that whilst uncomfortable, these physical symptoms are natural and normal. They are all the result of our body's natural survival reaction to threat. Our most primitive protective system, known as the lymbic system, leaps into action, preparing us for action, to fight or to 'fly' (run away): if these don't work, we may 'freeze', see below. Every one of the experiences listed above has a practical, physiological explanation. Far from signalling that you are about to keel over and die, these symptoms probably indicate that your nervous system is working extremely well, unless you have an underlying medical problem (see below).

What's happening?

The part of your brain known as the amygdala has perceived a potential danger. It has alerted another part of your brain known as the hypothalamus. The hypothalamus in turn activates your sympathetic nervous system to trigger your adrenals to release hormones. These hormones ready your body for an effective response. The hypothalamus has also stimulated your pituitary gland, which, in turn, activates the adrenals to produce cortisol. If you successfully deal with the threat, cortisol will gradually soothe the alarm, the amygdala will quieten down, and you'll feel your sense of relaxation and calm return.

It's much like being on a plane. The pilot is receiving information and making decisions, and will instruct cabin crew and passengers accordingly. If there's turbulence (the 'threat'), it makes sense for the message to go back to passengers to stop other activities and return to their seats, and for the crew to stop serving dinner. When the turbulence is over, the pilot will let people know, and the 'fasten seat belts sign' will be switched off.

The difference is that our limbic systems are nothing like as cool and rational as trained pilots - they are much more primitive, seeing situations as black-or-white *(it's either safe or it's dangerous - you're either with us or against us)* and they function at a deeper, faster level than conscious thought (of which more later). So perhaps it's a bit more like being flown by a very protective but rather excitable monkey: likely to be a bumpy ride!

Anyone facing a potential threat - from soldiers in battle,

to rugby players int the World Cup, to a speaker about to make a presentation, to a salesperson about to deal with an angry customer - or even anticipating a wonderful and exciting experience, like going to meet someone you're really attracted to, or waiting for the birthday girl to arrive when you've spent weeks planning a surprise party - is likely to feel these feelings, to some extent. Same nervous system, same route of preparation for best action.

So each physical symptom we experience has a very tangible, natural explanation. Knowing this can enable us to learn to accept the symptoms for the miracle of survival engineering they represent, rather than be alarmed by them.

Important note: *However, some serious physical conditions can produce symptoms that are similar or the same as anxiety symptoms. They may also be experienced as the side-effect of certain medication. So you may wish to consult a doctor if you are experiencing any of the symptoms for the first time, frequently, or in situations other than confined spaces.*

Physical symptoms explained

Heart-rate increases to pump blood as quickly as possible to the long muscles of our arms and legs, enabling us run faster or lift weights greater than we could possibly manage in a relaxed state. *Muscles tense*, ready to spring into action, which may lead to feelings of agitation if there is no possibility of springing. We may start shaking or trembling. If we're lying or sitting down, we may have an urge to get up. *Blood pressure increases*, forcing the blood around our systems, which may be experienced as pressure in the head and a pulse in the stomach. As this happens, we become *hot,* and *sweat* a lot, so we may have the feeling of wanting to get rid of everything, clothes, bags, other people, to reduce our body temperature and any further constriction, to be able to breathe and move more freely. Some of these anxiety symptoms may feel rather worse in confined spaces because of actual physical limitations; for example, it may be hard to pace up and down, a classic way to dissipate some of these effects.

Our *neck and eye muscles* become activated, and our *pupils dilate*; we become hyper vigilant, able to quickly scan our environment and better able to focus on possible threat. We *breathe faster*, and more *shallowly*, taking in the oxygen needed to fuel the muscles. This is highly effective if we're using our muscles to actually run or do battle, but if we're not, then it can lead to *hyperventilation*, to gasping, choking, feelings of breathlessness, weakness or dizziness, all of which feel distressing and uncomfortable. We may have the urge to sit or lie down, or feel we are about to collapse.

Our chests may ache as we heave for breath, compounding our fear that we are about to have a heart-attack. The worst that's actually likely to happen, if we continued to breathe very shallowly, is that we might faint, at which point normal breathing would resume. But for now, the important thing to know is that we need a bit more carbon dioxide, which can be readily achieved by slowly breathing in and out through your nose (reducing loss of CO_2), by breathing into a paper-bag for a few breaths (*see* p. 109), or even through your nose into your cupped hands (but not a plastic bag).

Digestion slows down and stops, just as we'd stop frying sausages and turn off the gas if we were suddenly called to the phone. This accounts for the dry mouth (saliva is not needed, so it also may be a bit hard to speak), stomach churning and queasiness. *Diarrhoea* or sensations of wanting to empty the bladder and bowels are created by blood leaving the digestive organs to go to muscles designed for escape, and also has the effect of making the body lighter for quicker action. As our bodies prepare for action, blood is also flowing away to our muscles, so our skin becomes *cold and pale*.

If the threat is perceived as extreme, if we can't 'fly' or 'fight', then we may go into *'freeze'* mode, like a rabbit in the headlights or a mouse 'playing dead' when it gets caught by a cat. It's not clear exactly how freezing happens, but the results are that there seem to be contradictory impulses jammed in the system. We may feel paralysed: our muscles either become stiff and tense, or floppy. Our skin may be cold but appear flushed. Heart and respiration rates are mixed, pupils may be dilated or constricted. Our experience in this state may feel very unreal: we may 'dissociate', feel as if we are not present in ourselves, or have the sense that we are watching what is happening from a distance. Awareness of time and our environment changes; we may not notice pain, and we may not feel anything, even fear. It's as if we close down, go numb, tune out.

We don't have a choice about freezing, so there is no need to feel guilt or shame if this happens. It's a valuable defence that our limbic system creates when all else fails. However, research suggests that there may be a greater chance of developing post-traumatic stress disorder if we have dissociated, than if we 'fly' or 'fight'. PTSD will not necessarily undo itself of its own accord. The amygdala may stay switched on, alert to possible threat, and the body is kept in emergency mode, ready to act. This is a very draining experience (if you have had this experience, in a confined space or elsewhere, you may wish to look into one of the therapies that specifically help with this level of traumatic input - *see* p. 228, and Appendix B for symptoms, before you tackle claustrophobia itself). Perhaps the relatively high percentage of people who experience claustrophobia is explained by this. Could we know, innately, that being less free to 'fly' or 'fight' has the potential to push us deeper into this last-ditch survival mode?

Our emotional experience

Those of us who experience claustrophobia also share many similar emotional reactions - feeling -

Frightened, scared, terrified, sense of dread

Angry, frustrated

Feelings of hopelessness and despair

Wanting to scream

Urge to grab and hold onto someone else - and/or - loss of empathy for anyone else

Loss of perspective, frame of reference reduced to the immediate situation

Above all ... a desperate need to find a way out to open space, air and light

This is a very unpleasant collection of feelings, natural as they all are. It is no wonder we have an urge to avoid putting ourselves into a place where there is the possibility of feeling this way ever again. It's comforting to know that many people have these experiences, even though we wouldn't wish them on anyone: there's relief in feeling understood. None of us is alone in having these feelings, nor does it mean we are weak or flawed in some way. They are part of the normal spectrum of human reaction.

Our species survived by its members staying together. Our feeling of wanting to connect to others is deeply 'wired' into our primitive brains, so it's natural that we reach out even to strangers for reassurance, that we want to communicate our distress by screaming. This same urge will lead us to protect each other, especially people we care about. But equally, our brains are also 'wired' for individual survival. Sometimes people feel great shame for having pushed others aside, or temporarily abandoned children, when in the grips of claustrophobia.

Our mental experience

What's going on in our minds, when we experience the pangs of claustrophobia? Regrettably, not a lot ...

> Loss of focus and clarity of thought, racing thoughts
>
> Thinking we're going to lose control or die

This isn't very much! - unsurprisingly. Reduction in our ability to think when we click into 'fight or flight' mode is natural. It's what helps us react immediately to situations of danger, to pull our child out of the way of an oncoming car, makes us withdraw our hands if we touch something too hot. We don't have to think - that's why we've survived as a species, long before we got clever with words. When our limbic systems are in full survival mode, there's little if any 'higher brain' thinking activity going on.

However, in many dangerous situations, we need precisely that kind of thinking, to assess the danger, discriminate between fact and fantasy, and to decide what to do. The neo-cortex is the part of our brain where we can think, use logic, be rational, make cool decisions, problem-solve. It's certainly the part of the brain real pilots will be using, in the example above, highly trained as they are to know how to respond to simple turbulence, as well as more dangerous situations.

So a core 'task' in overcoming claustrophobia is to develop the relationship between our primitive systems and higher brain, to find ways to reduce our arousal levels, when there is no real danger to fight or fly from. Or if there is genuine threat, to retain sufficient arousal to be ready to act, whilst maintaining our ability to think.

What people who experience claustrophobia miss out on

There are, of course, limitations on the careers we may choose as people who experience claustrophobia. You're unlikely to find us as submariners, miners (*though see* p. 74) air cabin crew, London Underground or Channel Tunnel train drivers, fire fighters, prison personnel, warehouse staff, astronauts or in forensic services. We might find it hard to work back-stage in a theatre, in crowded busy kitchens with walk-in fridges, or as 'back of house' hotel staff who need to use lengthy, badly lit corridors and creaky service lifts. Of course personnel in any of these jobs may experience claustrophobia at some point in their lives, and find it difficult to continue doing their work without support.

Regrettably, because we feel we have to avoid the possibility of being trapped in small or enclosed spaces, we also miss out on a lot of other kinds of opportunities. Here are comments from contributors;

"Going out if it meant travelling on the underground"

"Going to a job interview if I knew that I would have to use a lift. I cannot get another job if it means using public transport to get there, or use a lift to get to the office"

"I have avoided travelling by Eurostar, because there have been delays in or around the Tunnel, and the prospect of being trapped in that way freaks me out!"

"I have turned down trips that might have involved claustrophobic stituations such as high-rise hotels, necessitating using the lifts. A trip to New York - don't you have to go under a river in a tunnel to get from the airport to the centre of town?!?"

"Going into caves, on boats and on the ghost-train, with my family"

"I've missed out on loads. Parties, conferences, sales, firework displays, parades, shopping etc, anywhere there is a crowd or might be a crowd"

"School outings, social occasions, holiday opportunities, museums, you name it"

"Camping, mud/grass/sleeping bags/close proximity. I feel excluded and like I am missing out every time".

What's it like to turn down invitations and opportunities because of being worried that a situation might arise that would lead to claustrophobia?

"It's like being disabled. To be marginalised is a familiar place for me, not necessarily what I want but comfortably familiar and irritating"

"Makes me feel reluctant to attempt diving again ... such a shame because the underwater world is just amazing"

"I was beginning to feel my life was withering away"

"I have travelled less as a result. This has left me feeling that if I don't conquer my fears, I will die with regrets"

Many people with families feel frustrated at being unable to go with their children into attractions on holidays, for example fairground rides, theatres, cinemas or the London Eye. They also feel regretful that family trips have to be planned around their need to avoid tunnels or closed methods of transport, sometimes incurring more travelling time or expense. Others felt that they had missed out on moving freely and being able to be spontaneous, and were worried that friends might stop inviting them.

On the other hand, some people wouldn't dream of turning down an invitation, and find ways of coping despite their fears.

"Never. Just suffered agony. My ex-husband worked in tunnels underground and insisted I went to the Christmas do. I went and panicked for about five hours but stayed. He would not let me come out but at least I didn't give in"

So should claustrophobia be considered a kind of disability?

Should architects, designers, planners, businesses, employers, services, shops and so on take claustrophobia into account?

"They should: I think everyone, surely, would become stressed to the point of panic if enclosed in a tiny space for long enough"

"Haha! - I've a permanent bump on my head from butting this wall"

"It is a disability in the sense that I would be unable to use some facilities such as lifts, or the public toilets on streets which have automatic doors"

"No, I think it's a psychological response that can be treated, although I do think space and place design should take it into account - most places that trigger claustrophobia are unsafe"

"In extreme cases it is clearly a disability, but I don't see how, nor the need for taking it into account"

"I don't see it as a disability. It has not stopped me doing anything as long as buildings have stairs as well as lifts. There are so many good treatments"

"It could be considered a disability, but in the end it's down to the individual"

"In some ways it is a disability, as it restricts one's freedom of movement. And bearing in mind that claustrophobia is a relatively common condition, I do feel strongly that architects and planners should take it into account. Many trains, public loos and some cars could do with a massive re-think/re-design ... If the air-conditioning malfunctions in summer on trains with no windows that can be opened, the situation becomes quite unnecessarily intolerable for passengers. I've raised this with railway personnel, but I've received unhelpful answers to the effect that the air-con is usually very efficient! - this does nothing to reassure me"

How do you feel about experiencing claustrophobia?

Knowing that we experience claustrophobia is upsetting and

frustrating for many people, though others accept it. Some have compassion for themselves, and are still hopeful of improvement.

"I feel really annoyed it's like this; it limits my life. And it affects my family, so I feel guilty and like a burden to them when we go on holiday, for example. I miss out on joint experiences, like going into caves or boats on canals. Unfortunately therapy hasn't helped"

"It's a feature of my personality, like being vegetarian. It's been there for the whole of my adult life. It might not be the best part (of me) but it's there. I'm sure that's why I put off dealing with it"

"I feel very despondent. I feel that I am letting myself down when I am unable to cope in a claustrophobic situation. I feel I should be able to cope but am behaving in a cowardly way if I have to run away"

"I'm irritated that my own responses, irrespective of the facts, might limit my activities. But I know I'm not alone in my fears, and I do know the source and sometimes the cure"

"This shouldn't have happened to me, I'm a mature professional woman, I don't do panic"

"I felt frightened, and at times helpless, and also angry that it was affecting me the way it did. ... I felt it was a great blight on my life. I could not understand why it had come about. I felt it would never leave me"

"I just have to lump it"

"It makes life more expensive; I can only fly if I go business class"

"I felt depressed, diminished as a person and hopeless. I think ' why me? 'I wish with all my heart that I didn't (experience claustrophobia)*"*

"I can totally understand why I feel this way. It's irritating, but understandable"

"It's just one of those things. I'd rather not be claustrophobic"

"It seems ridiculous and I would rather be in control. I do feel there is a deep-seated reason for it"

"I think there can be no phobia as ineradicable as this one: because surely everyone would become stressed to the point of panic if enclosed in a tiny space long enough"?

"I'm very annoyed that it limits my life"

"I don't think I used to feel this way, it is something I have developed with age so I think my mind has control over it"

"I'm sometimes 'in denial' about it when I interact with other people, as I chose who to be open with (and vice versa, who not to tell). But I reassure myself by the knowledge that there are many others 'out there' who are also claustrophobic"

"Feel a bit silly, but aware it's a common thing"

"Just something about me that I have to deal with and learn to manage

"Frustration that after all those years the bad experience of being shut in an upstairs cupboard haunts me"

"I feel very frustrated and different from other people. It's been a very trying experience: but I feel good about overcoming it to a point"

Telling other people

People who experience claustrophobia often feel deeply ashamed of our fears, and hide our anxiety by avoiding situations. But sometimes we feel we want or have to tell our partners, families, friends, or even strangers. Sometimes the message is direct and immediate:

"I've never used those words - "I'm claustrophobic" - it's usually just "I've got to get out of here NOW!".

Sometimes we tell others in order to get the help we need to manage particular situations, or to explain our avoidance.

"I've had to explain why I don't go in the tube, and I had to tell the staff at the hospital when I went for an MRI"

"I've told my wife to explain why I need to avoid certain situations. The reaction was a gradual understanding of what this means"

"I frequently have to explain why I'm not taking lifts"

When we tell others that we experience claustrophobia, we get a variety of responses.

"Most of my family and friends are supportive and kind, or they tell me to "get over it". There's often laughter. My children are the worst. I got stuck in a loo in a designer dress shop in Milan, and I was panicking, calling for help, and I could hear my children laughing, "Mummy's locked in the toilet!".

"People have no difficulty understanding the stress of being trapped in a tube train"

"I've mostly had well-meaning offers to accompany me (into lifts). When I have declined, I have been given the impression that they felt I was over-reacting to the situation and I would be fine if they were with me"

"Initially I felt very embarrassed telling people, I imagined they'd see me as weak, especially younger colleagues at work, although nobody said anything. But I've got used to telling people, and I'm more confident to say it now. I recognise that a person's reaction is much more about them than it is about me - decent people will always try to help I think. And it helps that I've overcome some of my difficulties and feel good about that"

"My husband tried to be supportive but he did not understand my experiences and sometimes got fed up with the effects

of them. Friends were mostly supportive, but one said I
should 'get myself sorted out'"

Some people feel comfortable to be very upfront about their claustrophobia, and by telling others, find help and support.

"I tell everyone. Most people are very kind. I can go in a
lift only with other people and when I tell they are more
than willing to help".

But conversely other people feel it's more helpful *not* to share their experience:

"I try my best to deny and control it (mind over matter) and
saying it out loud may make it an issue and beyond my
control"

"... I don't feel able to 'out' myself to everyone I know for fear
of being considered neurotic, of being misunderstood or
of my feelings being trivialised"

I am very grateful to those people who've been kind enough to share their experiences in this book. It is my profound belief that by doing so, they have enabled other people to feel less alone with their experience. It's a valuable contribution.

The opposite of feeling trapped

Finally, what do people who experience claustrophobia really enjoy? Where do we feel most relaxed, happy and free? These are the situations we love. These are the ones that make us feel wonderful.

These are the ones we need to spend more time relishing.

"Calm, happy, at peace and in control. I try my best to create this when it is not happening naturally"

"Feeling calm, relaxed and safe"

"Home, my garden, being with friends"

"Being in the open air, anywhere, town or country or at the seaside. Anywhere that is not confined"

"Being on a deserted beach, providing I can cross the sand in a wheelchair"

"Running, walking the dogs, cycling, being in mountains"

"Fresh air, walking by the sea, alone or with others, or on open downland, or by a river. The sense of space and consequent freedom; a feeling of being 'at one' with the elements; the enjoyment of beautiful countryside/seascapes, and the feeling of escape from responsibilities"

"Both obviously and literally not being enclosed. Feeling 'planted' to the earth - in touch with myself and my surroundings, eyes wide open, all sense available to take in the environment. I can and do recreate this - it could be my back garden or on a walk, or it could be something like a conversation where I feel connected to another."

Chapter 4

What causes claustrophobia?

If we take 'being' or 'feeling claustrophobic' to mean *getting anxious in or about confined spaces to a greater degree than the situation actually warrants*, could it be that some people are born with a tendency to have this experience?

Did we inherit it, or learn it from our parents? Did something happen to sensitise us and make us anxious about small, enclosed spaces? Could we be feeling emotionally trapped in our lives, and be projecting that feeling into confined spaces? And in any case, is it really so irrational to be afraid of being trapped?

Was I born with it?
Some people have a profound sense that they have 'always' felt claustrophobic, as if the anxiety is an ancient part of themselves, almost a 'given'.

"I've been claustrophobic forever"

" I think I was born like this"

"Claustrophobia is such a deep part of me, I couldn't imagine life not feeling like that".

Could we be born claustrophobic? Could we, for example, have a more heightened sensitivity to reduced oxygen in the air or to reduced oxygen movement, for some reason? Underlying health difficulties, such as heart or respiratory diseases, can produce symptoms that may be triggered more quickly by the stress created by being confined. As such, it's always wise to seek medical advice if you have experienced unusual symptoms and want to eliminate the possibility of physiological causes before trying experiments in confined space. But there doesn't seem to be conclusive research at present to suggest that people without underlying health problems who experience claustrophobia are physiologically different from those who don't. Whilst sometimes people who experience claustrophobia also have parents who experience claustrophobia, this could be more a matter of learning the response rather than inheriting it in our genetic make-up.

Learning starts extremely early. Some of our deepest held beliefs and attitudes, and thus anxieties, may have arisen in response to things that happened to us long before our conscious memories began. 'Re-birthing' therapists, for example, believe that claustrophobia can be traced back to birth trauma. Such trauma might include being trapped with the umbilical cord around our necks, distress during a long or complicated labour, being a breech birth and so on. Thoughts like

"Small, tight spaces will hurt me or are dangerous"
"If I am trapped, I'll die"
or
"If I get trapped, there's nothing I can do to help myself".

- *might* have been formed at the time of the birth trauma, not in so many words, but in a wordless, body-based way. This central belief of re-birthing therapy (*see* p. 240) can't be proved, but it may help some people to believe that a birth trauma was the cause of their present anxiety. Bronwen Astor, a psychoanalyst, says:

> *"It can be very reassuring for people to know that something might actually have happened to them, that it's not just something in their imagination. You can't change what happened, but the important thing to know is that you survived. There's no need to be overwhelmed now, because the worst is behind you".*

We can't know for sure, even if our mothers tell us that *"Yes, you did get stuck, and yes, it was very traumatic"*. But one thing is certain. Neuroscientific research clearly shows that our bodies hold many secrets, at a depth that our conscious minds cannot yet reach. Our bodies can't lie! It's our minds that are not always expert in working out the truths our bodies are trying to tell us. So it's possible that if we feel we've 'always' been claustrophobic, it could be because the 'cause' was too early to remember.

The best we can do, when our bodies register fear, whatever the reason, is to be accepting and compassionate, and find ways to look after ourselves, just as we would with someone else who was afraid. It is no time to be judgmental, dismissive, or critical.

At the other end of the birth spectrum, several women in my research said that they first experienced claustrophobia when they became pregnant, or more frequently, after they had children. Once they become mothers, women often become aware of both new responsibilities and the potential dangers in the world, in a way that they might not have been before having children. It's possible that these two aspects of awareness could combine in a heightened anxiety about small or enclosed spaces, and trigger a claustrophobic panic.

I feel I've learnt to be claustrophobic from other people

"My mother avoided closed-in spaces. In the war, she would never go in an air-raid shelter, she preferred to be outside. My paternal grandparents fled from Poland in the pogroms of the late 1800s, maybe something came down the line from that. I do feel there is a deep-seated reason for it".

"My father was very claustrophobic. I remember feeling scared and going quiet when he got tense. He would just have to get out, whatever the situation, and there was no talking about it afterwards, it was very taboo. I didn't really understand what he was experiencing then. Now I do!"

"My eldest daughter is claustrophobic. She has the same fears as I do although I don't think I 'infected' her the same way as my mother did me"

"I never used to find crowds a problem eg shopping or clubbing. But I became aware that different people who were pushing my wheelchair becoming panicky, and I found that curious. I don't remember a specific moment that I also began to feel it!"

"I had an interesting moment once getting into a lift. I suddenly started to panic. I remember very clearly thinking, "Whoa, f***, that is my mother's stuff - there is no way you are going to start getting fearful of lifts" ... and hey presto, I was sorted! Almost mystical and instant and lasting."

"My mother was claustrophobic. It didn't affect me directly, but she tended to be over-protective of me and discouraged risk-taking. She avoided claustrophobic situations - trains, lifts and so on".

As children, we are very affected by the ways in which our immediate family feel and behave. Their anxieties and responses shape how we view the world, for good or ill. Naturally, it's important that we learn from the previous generation, otherwise we would be constantly re-inventing the wheel, or at least having to find out that fire burns, bees sting, cats bite, and so on, by painful trial-and-error. And we also need to be pointed in the direction of the good things, to learn that flowers smell lovely, cats' fur is soft to the touch, that we'll get a huge sense of pride if we balance all the way along a wall (and that, actually, small spaces are just small spaces, and that hot feeling is just a hot feeling which will go away soon).

On the other hand, it's of vital importance that we find out about life for ourselves, by direct contact with real-world experience. If we don't, we'll always be at one remove from reality, living a life based on other people's assessments. If we are to become independent, then our parents need to give us a lot of permission to find out for ourselves, hoping they can keep us safe enough while we do so.

This is often a challenging aspect of parenting, requiring parents to bite their tongues and keep their anxieties to themselves. Probably no-one gets the balance between protection and letting go exactly right all the time.

So if we have a parent, or parents who experienced claustrophobia, then it is likely that we could have learnt our phobia from them in at least three ways. The first is that we will witness our parents' anxiety about confined spaces, which may put an unconscious association - confined space = danger - into our young minds *(after all, Daddy was right that it hurts when the cat bites)*.

Secondly, our experience of confined spaces may actually be more limited than it might be for children of adults who didn't experience claustrophobia, because we couldn't go alone to the places our parents avoided. We may have received explicit warnings *"Don't go in that cave, the sea might rise and you might get stuck"*. Some of the warnings might have been accurate, but if they were based on our parents' phobic fear, we may have limited our exploration based on a mis-assessment. Their avoidance may have meant we didn't get the chance to find out for ourselves that maybe those places weren't so bad after all, at least for us. So we grow up with some of our beliefs un-tested by reality, and too scared - and possibly too loyal - to check them out.

And thirdly, our parents' fear itself may have created difficult feelings for us, which were hard to bear alone and which we also come to associate with confined spaces. For example, if you are a small child in a lift with a panicking parent, you may have felt anxious, not so much about the lift but about seeing Mummy getting upset. And you may have felt even worse if your young attempts to soothe her didn't work. Children want to help their parents because they love them, not just to feel safe themselves, so anxiety may be compounded by guilt at not being able to do so.

As an adult, your present anxiety about lifts may be more to do with those feelings, than about the lift itself. As the lift doors open, it may be hard to work out where your uneasiness is coming from, if you have no conscious memory of how your mother reacted. You just know you don't want to experience those helpless, out-of-control, vulnerable feelings again.

And whilst some people who experience claustrophobia feel they 'learnt' to be claustrophobic by living with another person

- often a parent - who had this anxiety, there are many people who live with or are close to others who experience claustrophobia who don't develop this anxiety themselves. So there are likely to be many other factors at work - personality, including resilience factors, *see* p. 165) pre-existing coping mechanisms (for example if the parent developed claustrophobia when the child was older) relationship to the parent or person experiencing claustrophobia, availability of other supportive relationships, empathy and imagination, or lack of these, roles acquired through birth order or gender, and so on.

A trauma caused my phobia

"I believe that my claustrophobia was caused by particular events, that it was physically and psychologically initiated. It's not intrinsic to my nature"

Some people are confident they can track back to a particular incident or situation that has caused a lifetime's struggle with claustrophobic feelings, or something more recent that has had a profound effect. During the event, the person had the experience of being physically trapped in some way, experiencing it as very distressing or frightening.

There are many ways of dealing with shock and trauma during and after such an event. However 'well' or 'badly' we coped at the time of the trauma, our way of coping afterwards was to avoid getting into that precise situation again, for fear of re-experiencing the horrible feelings, or worse. Then we may have started finding other situations of a related kind difficult. Then we may begin to avoid those. Then we don't even want to think about them. We gradually shrink our world, by avoiding more and more places and challenges.

Here are some contributors' thoughts about what happened for them:

"Travelling on underground trains triggered it for me, especially after fainting on one occasion"

"I think being physically disabled has definitely impacted my sense of feeling trapped and unable to escape"

"Being 'stuck' in a toilet with a stiff lock: several memories of this"

"When about eight years old travelling on a train through France, I was playing in the corridor and the train went into a tunnel. It was pitch black. This gave me such a shock that I have been scared of the dark every since. This in itself did not cause me to become claustrophobic but I feel that it "conditioned" me to be susceptible to phobias. Then in my 30's I had to travel in the back of a two-door car with another person and two large suitcases. I felt extremely claustrophobic. From then on I became acutely aware of my surroundings and rapidly came to fear all enclosed spaces, for example, underground trains, lifts and so on"

"There was a narrow corridor into the museum. It was hot and there were lots of people to go in. I couldn't see the end of the corridor as there was bend in it. I tried several times to go through to the museum but failed"

"My sibling wrapping me in blankets. There was no malice involved, it was all fun until the claustrophobia started"

Some people have had the misfortune of claustrophobia being triggered during medical or dental treatment:

"I hated the mask (anaesthetic) put over my face at the dentist or in hospital"

"As a very young child I had to have teeth extracted and a gas mask was forced onto my face and held there until I lost consciousness. That was very distressing"

"My sister had an MRI scan and it was terrible. She'd never had a problem with claustrophobia before, but I think the whole thing about being in pain, the hospital setting, that awful small tunnel you have to go in, it all added up. And unfortunately the staff weren't sympathetic, it was ghastly"

Some people feel that the trauma that caused their phobia was not so much an event as something that someone else did to them, remembering acts of real unkindness or thoughtlessness on the part of the people caring for them. The events themselves seem traumatic enough; in these examples, it's especially easy to imagine that the impression left on small children would be stronger because of the hostility or insensitivity from the adults involved.

"I was tricked into a walk-in fridge by the under-chef when I was waitressing. He actually shut me in. I was absolutely terrified. I can't imagine how anyone could do such a thing"

"My sister was claustrophobic to a point, but not as bad as me. Our mother was a very cruel woman and locked us in cupboards. She put me in a coal cupboard and I remember screaming in fear. I was about eight. I am sure this was the beginning of severe claustrophobia"

"When I was about three years old a housekeeper/nanny used to close me inside a large garden hammock by putting a tarpaulin cover over it if she thought I misbehaved"

Is claustrophobia inevitable, after a traumatic event?

No. Not everyone who experiences trauma will go on to become claustrophobic. We all have different coping mechanisms, support structures of varying strengths, and what will work for one person may not be effective for another. Research indicates that how stressed someone was at the time of the trauma is related to the likelihood of developing post-traumatic stress disorder (the more stressed the more likely). Phobia only develops when we begin to avoid the thing we fear. If someone is afraid, but is able to support him or her self to go back into a situation where an accident or incident occurred, as many Londoners did after the 7/7 bombs in the tube system, then he or she is not creating a mind-set for the development of a phobia.

Some people may not have a strong fear response at the time of a traumatic event, or even if they did, they were subsequently extremely well supported. My mother, for example, was 'bombed in' as a young girl, in a WWII London air-raid shelter, trapped underground for an hour and a half in what many people would imagine would be terrifying circumstances - no light, dusty air, completely dependent on other people to be rescued. She remembers being very frightened, but that the adults with her remained calm whist they waited for rescue: although her grandmother was furious that the blackberrry-and-apple she'd just cooked might go to waste! Afterwards, even though the family home was destroyed (along with the pudding) my mother simply remembers a huge sense of relief, which seems to have washed away the previous sense of fear. And whilst she's not keen on the idea of being trapped again (which she has been, in a lift) she's certainly not claustrophobic.

Trauma can be cumulative, or the depth or intensity of the trauma experienced can be too much for a particular person on a particular day, even having survived other events. Everyone probably has a 'tipping point', as far as fear is concerned. It could be that we simply haven't known how to manage the level of fear we've experienced, or we've lost confidence in our ability to do so. It might be that we didn't or don't have the kind of support we need. Or it could be that we generally manage difficult feelings by avoiding situations that provoke them (see below). Whatever the reason, telling ourselves we *'should'* be able to cope or forcing ourselves solely with will-power is unlikely to get us all immediately making bookings on Eurostar. If it were that easy, claustro*phobia* per se wouldn't exist (and this book would not have been written).

But noticing how people - including ourselves - cope with frightening situations, *is* of enormous benefit. It is highly likely that people who experience claustrophobia have had to manage fear and trauma in other areas of our lives, and have done so successfully. The fear is the same fear. What we need to understand is why confined spaces have so far proved a greater challenge.

Could fear of being trapped be more an emotional issue?

Claustrophobia may have been started with a trauma in a confined space, but there may be deeper reasons why we avoid such places. We may be transferring or projecting difficult feelings from another situation: we may have problems with feeling attached to other people, and general feelings of insecurity in the world: we may have developed avoidance as a primary way of coping with our lives.

PROJECTION

If we have suppressed or repressed our emotions about particular experiences because they were too painful or confusing, then our feelings of frustration, anger, grief, impotence and anxiety may become *projected* out onto the external world of confined spaces. If we're already 'a bit' claustrophobic, the problem can get worse. We may worry about getting trapped in confined spaces in the real world because inside we're feeling 'emotionally trapped'.

> *"I went to India just as a major relationship was ending. My bag got stolen, with my passport, camera, everything. I had a panic attack in the middle of a huge crowd at a temple and then felt trapped and panicky on the way home. The claustrophobia started then, but I'm sure the loss of the relationship was the big thing"*

> *"Once I had children in my late 20's my feelings of claustrophobia increased, but became very pronounced after suffering several bereavements (of close family members) in three years".*

Some people who experience claustrophobia in confined spaces also find other situations claustrophobic - time commitments, deadlines, intense relationships, arguments, sex, intimacy and much besides. This may be more about your internal world than it is to do with a particular event.

> *"The first time I felt truly claustrophobic I'd had a really unpleasant lunch with my mother ... Afterwards I was unable to get on the tube"*

INSECURITY AND NOT FEELING ATTACHED

As tiny babies, one of our primary instincts is to form attachments with the adults caring for us. If you have loving adults who also have the desire to build that bond with the real you, by attuning to your needs, making sure you don't get overly anxious or distressed, by sharing their joy with you and supporting your excitement in the world, you are likely to grow up feeling secure in yourself, with other people, and in life. A template has been established that relationships are beneficial, and the world in general a good place.

You may be the kind of person who has solid networks of family, friends, neighbours and colleagues, to turn to in the good and bad times. You know you can both ask for help and support, and, in your turn, provide it for other people. Your support network would help you, in person or in your mind's eye, if you were in a confined space. You know that when you're separated from them, people in your network will '*hold you in mind*', just as so many people around the world '*held*' BBC journalist Alan Johnston in mind when he was kidnapped in 2007. They won't forget or abandon you. Your template of positive relationships probably allows you to remember that support services will always try to find you if you get stuck somewhere, and that out in the world there are many people who wish you well, even though they haven't even met you.

Peter Levine, in his helpful book *Healing Trauma: A Pioneering Program for Restoring the Wisdom of Your Body* (SoundsTrue 2005) gives us an affirmation from the Native American tradition, that seems to underpin the attitude of secure people:

"I give thanks for help unknown, already on its way"

However, if, for whatever reason, a baby doesn't form secure attachments in his early life, if his carers are absent, unreliable, neglectful or even abusive, he - or she - may develop a template that says relationships cannot be trusted. This baby growing up may feel insecure in and about himself, with other people and about life. He may not know how to make connections with others that will be satisfying and enriching for himself or for them. He may feel he has to take care of himself, always stay in control because everyone else might let him down. He may feel isolated even when there are others nearby, and avoid interaction even though he wants it, or reject others before they reject him. His insecurity and feeling of isolation may manifest as fear of being out of control, of being trapped, and this fear transferred to confined spaces.

Others find that being cut off from other people is in itself a frightening experience, one they would rather avoid. If someone has a deep-seated anxiety about being alone, it may result from her early childhood experiences that left the impression that her needs for affection, warmth and care were not important to other people. Maybe their needs were given precedence. This will profoundly affect how she would come to feel about relationships. At some level, she may believe that '*out of sight*' means '*out of mind*', and that if she is separated from other people, she will be forgotten and not cared about. She may have even less belief in strangers caring whether she lives or dies. If this baby, grown up to be a woman, experiences anxiety about confined spaces, it may reinforce fears she's had for a very long time.

This is terrifying prospect. If this has been her experience, as an adult she may arrange her life so that she is always with other people. Small and enclosed places may trigger the unconscious fear of being alone, lonely, helpless and forgotten. She won't consciously make the connection when she step into a lift, or hesitate before she locks the loo door or enter the walk-in fridge, but some of the old terrors may be lurking in the flood of claustrophobic panic she experiences (I often wonder if there might be someone locked inside the electronic street loos that are in many cities now - how would we know?). She may not want to go too far from home, or too far from the people she knows. (In this way, claustrophobia can almost begin to verge on agoraphobia, but perhaps that is another story).

"I guess the diving situation was totally impersonal: nobody knew me or gave two hoots about what I thought or felt. A bit like the times I have felt claustrophobic (when I'm not diving); if I'm hemmed in and crowded, particularly if the crowd is unapproachable or intimidating"

AVOIDANCE AS MANAGING DISTRESS

Some people's upbringing is such that they learn to use avoidance as a global coping mechanism for many different kinds of emotional experience. This may be because *'sweeping things under the carpet'*, avoidance, silence and stoicism rather than problem-solving were the strategies most employed by their parents and families. Or it may be the opposite. There have been such strong emotion displayed in the home with painful and disruptive consequences that the child may have 'decided' at an earlier age to behave very differently. In either case, the avoidance implicit in claustrophobia may simply be the most familiar reaction when times get tough.

Some people find that not only do they experience claustrophobia in confined space, but also feel a kind of 'emotional claustrophobia' when circumstances have a confining element about them, and may use avoidance in such situations as well. In my work on procrastination, I've found many people who experience claustrophobia- like symptoms just before a confrontation, deadline or a major decision, sometimes even before simply getting a project started. Watch the scene with Hugh Grant as Charles just before he goes into the church to marry 'Duckface' in the *film Four Weddings and a Funeral*, and you will see a perfect example of emotional claustrophobia just about contained in the face of a major decision.

"I have occasional 'social' claustrophobia. This means that after either prolonged or intense time with other people either in a business or social group I need to get away and be in my own space"

"Linked to my procrastination, I can feel pretty hemmed in by deadlines and the pressure of having to deliver creative excellence. This makes me avoidant"

To begin to reverse that process, to stop avoiding, may bring all kinds of other unresolved issues closer to the surface, and disproportionately 'load' the work being done on returning to confined spaces. On a more hopeful note, any work done in other areas of life on finding ways to engage with problems and distress, rather than avoiding, will have positive knock-on effects on working with claustrophobia about confined space.

If we start to re-visit confined spaces, real or emotional, complex feelings may emerge, and we may need time, space and support to work through what is happening in our inner worlds. 'Treatments' that solely focus on the mental and behavioural aspects of helping you 'back into the saddle' - back into using small and confined spaces - may not be able to offer this level of support. Experimenting with going back is a way to find out what depth of support we need.

Environmental sensitivity or imagination?

Finally, could those of us who experience claustrophobia be more sensitive to our environment than other people?   More imaginative?   Some of the contributors recognise the possibility:

"I wonder if practical people don't make the same empathic leaps as imaginative people do, they don't get caught up in imaginative things. They live in a more material 'real' world, and are less affected by their imaginings - for better or worse"

"Some tunnels, especially the Severn Tunnel ... (are difficult). I think this dates back to a very bad accident in the Tunnel, involving a number of fatalities. This set my imagination racing and made me realise the potential risks of travelling through the Tunnel, bearing in mind the current overcrowding on the railways and cost- cutting"

Whatever attributes those of us who have experienced claustrophobia have, the key question is how we choose to use them. If we have a heightened sensitivity to potential danger, for whatever reason, and we use it appropriately, we may be able to keep ourselves and others safe on the few occasions the danger is real (*see* p. 87 *and* p. 167 for the genuine contribution we can make). If we have strong imaginative faculties, we may be able to do the same.

But if we become over-focused on danger, see definite threat where none or only a very slim possibility exists, we are more likely to be terrorising ourselves and others by crying wolf. And that can mean that our confidence in our ability to assess risk and trust our assessment of other situations will also be de-stabilised.

Is claustrophobia completely irrational?

This is an important question, if we want to overcome our claustrophobia. We need to know if we are aiming for a zero reaction to a confined space, or something else. Could there be a rational element in our 'phobic anxiety' about small and enclosed spaces, that won't - or shouldn't - be wished away?

BEING AFRAID OF SMALL SPACES IS A RATIONAL HUMAN REACTION

First of all, let's consider the fear on which our phobia is based. The fear of being *trapped* in a small space has its roots in reality. After all, we are animals. If we were in a closed environment with no oxygen, we would eventually die. Watch someone catching a spider in a glass, a fish in a net, attempting to put a cat into a cage to take to the vet, or a baby trying to push a hat off its face and then try telling yourself that your own fear of confined small spaces is wholly, totally, and completely irrational. It's not. We have an animal reflex to reject being confined and in danger of losing oxygen. If we lose that reflex, we'd be in trouble.

In addition, we are far less able to defend ourselves in a confined space than we might be able to on open ground, where we could at least try running from potential threat.

And because we are biologically wired to fight or run away (or freeze) when we get anxious or are under threat, the problem is compounded when our exits seem blocked in very confined space. Cats voluntarily secrete themselves in small snug spaces, judged by the width of their whiskers, but they protest immediately if they can't leave or if an attempt is made to touch them if retreat is impossible. Unwanted confinement leads them to hiss, scratch and attack anything that comes near. As animals, we are mobilised to act in the face of threat, with all the bodily signs of arousal that adrenaline creates. In a small and confined space, our *inability* to do so is compounded. Animals will resist this highly unnatural situation, tooth, claw and angry snarl, if they can. Our spontaneous swearing and frantic, manic attempts to open stuck lift doors or stuck zips on high-necked clothes are no different.

And if our bodies react from a deeply primitive core, to restricted movement and air flow, our minds will equally reject entrapment, at both primitive and more sophisticated levels. It's true that a baby can lie placidly in a metal cot under earthquake rubble for far longer than a child or adult. The baby can't panic because it 'thinks' it will die; it has no words to create such an image or voice such a fear. But the baby will protest if it is left alone for too long, and become overwhelmed with distress. The innate need for attachment, for contact with and comfort from another person, is wired far deeper in its brain than the words to express it.

But adults understand the potential implications, and to feel such terror and not be able to escape, is horrendous. We are scared that our feelings, emotional or physical, will be unbearable. We imagine that an accident or attack may happen, and that we may die. But we are equally worried about being stuck in perpetual agony, without assistance; and we almost don't know which is worse. This is true terror, and it is hardly surprising we avoid re-experiencing that feeling. The fear of being buried alive, abandoned, runs through all ages, and through all cultures. When the BBC journalist Alan Johnston was released by his kidnappers in the Lebanon in 2007, he described the appalling experience of being held in solitary confinement, in the dark, as just that: being buried alive, with the massive fear of being forgotten whilst the world moved on. He called for all hostages and people imprisoned without trial to be remembered and sought out. (The Times, London, July 4th, 2007)

So to dismiss our dislike and distrust of confined spaces as wholly irrational - as phobias are often assumed to be - is to suggest we can - or should - switch off our animal and human awareness to the potential dangers of those spaces. I believe this is a unhealthy and unnatural thing to do. And as a society, it's surely unhealthy for us to turn a blind eye to the ways in which technology can create new traps for real flesh-and-blood human beings (*see* Part 2).

But we are not going to get trapped and die in every small and confined space we enter. Nor is it likely that our feelings, however horrendous, will prove fatal. What we need to do is discriminate between the rational element of our fears, and the phobic.

FEAR CAN BE HEALTHY AND HELPFUL

Of course in some closed situations, the potential for danger is publicly acknowledged, and we are advised to keep our 'antennae' switched on. We are positively encouraged to make sure we know how to leave the building by Health & Safety officers at the start of every conference, every public meeting. On a plane, we're advised *"to locate the exit nearest to us"*; we're trained to know the location of the fire exits where we work, we're invited to check out routes of escape on trains and in hotels, and not to leave baggage unattended.

Those of us who experience claustrophobia are often model citizens in this respect. I used to travel frequently by plane with a particular friend, always making sure to read the safety card. On one occasion, however, I decided that maybe I was being a little neurotic, and that I would risk not reading the card, just this once. To my surprise my friend looked at me with alarm.

"Why aren't you reading the card?" she asked.
"I rely on you to know what it says!"

People who experience claustrophobia are already sensitised to our environment, and don't need to be told to look for the nearest available exit. We've independently found several options already (and we've seen that one of them is slightly blocked). We wouldn't park in front of gates, turn on our car-engines on the ferry before the boat has docked, put our heads in plastic bags, over-fill the lift or sit in the aisles of theatres. We just don't, because we've already thought ahead (often very far ahead) and can see the potential log-jam, or danger.

So we have a useful social function, and I believe the contribution we can genuinely make will become more significant if systems of electronic control in vehicles and buildings become more usual, and if the more faceless, impersonal aspects of bureaucracy continue to grow. Noticing our fear, using adrenaline to move us into action to escape or to deal with potential danger, can be very constructive.

Fear is not our problem. It's there to alert us to danger, and to move us to save ourselves and the people we care about. What we need to do is to find ways of relating to our fear, so that we are not helpless or disempowered when it appears. We need to be able to feel our fear, assess it, choose the most appropriate response to the situation that has provoked the fear, and then act on it.

WHEN IRRATIONAL RESPONSES DEVELOP

For real safety (and there will never be hundred percent guarantees), we not only need to notice our environment, *we need accurate powers of assessment to make decisions about what we notice.* We need to be able to discriminate between the definitely dangerous, the potentially dangerous, the as-safe-as-is-reasonable-but-not-at-all-pleasant and the 99.999 % safe.

So it is true that flying is dangerous - but statistically far less so than crossing the road. Lifts do get stuck - but far, far, *far* less frequently than the number of lift journeys taken per day, and the number of people being hurt because they were stuck in a lift is even tinier. There have been accidents and incidents of terrorist attacks on trains, buses and the underground, but the number of times this has happened compared to the number of journeys taken each day and each year is microscopic. Has anyone ever died because they were stuck in a cupboard-under-the-stairs? And I have to confess that even though I've been too scared to lock the door, I've never seen reports of the person who was hurt because he or she was stuck in a loo, especially not in a restaurant.

So, and it's a huge so, the *irrational* element of our fear as people who experience claustrophobia creeps in when aspects of a new situation remind us in some way of dangers we've experienced before, or heard about. We mis-read our response. We think we're afraid because the situation is dangerous. Our own panic panics us. We take our compounded level of fear as the risk-indicator - as in,

If I feel really *frightened, it must be because*
The Thing I'm frightened of is really *dangerous*

We begin to translate the *possibilities* of entrapment into *probabilities*, when there is no evidence for this, and then, as the phobia develops, into *certainties*, against which we feel we have to defend ourselves, usually by avoidance. Our powers of assessment are not as developed as they need to be, or if they were once developed, they have regressed.

However our fears developed in the first place, they are maintained and deepened in three ways. Firstly, by generalising from actual experience, or news of accidents and incidents, to believing we will inevitably have the same experience again. Secondly, our fear leads us to distort the effects of entrapment, which in most cases, are unpleasant, distressing, but rarely fatal. And thirdly, by avoiding the situations we fear, subsequently even avoiding talking and thinking about those situations, our theories that we won't survive remain untested by real-world experience.

Our challenge, as people who experience claustrophobia is to disentangle our strong associations of fear to confined spaces, so that we can approach each situation on its actual merits, including any real threats to safety. *We need to learn or restore the ability to think and feel, and be fully present in our bodies, all at the same time.* Then we can be of greater assistance both to ourselves and to others, should the need arise.

The development of claustrophobia is not deliberate or conscious. We don't wake up one day and think -

> *What shall I do today? - Gardening? Go for a walk? Visit friends? No, I know, I'll frighten myself by thinking up some awful scenario about being trapped and helpless in the back of a three-door car sitting behind two huge men who make it impossible for me to get out in the event of the car going into water.*

- although presumably the makers of horror films have this kind of thought on a Sunday morning. Perhaps we could all have alternative careers as disaster movie script-writers! (*and see imagination above, and on* p. 158).

Claustrophobia is not something anyone would wish for, or wish on anyone else. It's a response that develops: some people have a very clear sense of when and why their claustrophobia began, and others really don't. Some people don't mind that they don't know, and others feel frustrated. What we do all know is that for whatever reason, we feel anxious in and about confined spaces, in the here-and-now, and that these feelings can be profoundly unpleasant.

But it is in the here-and-now that we can help ourselves most. So we can all make progress with overcoming our claustrophobia, even if we don't know precisely what caused it. And that has to be good news.

Part 2

Is it getting worse?

Chapter 5

The past, present and future of confined space

Many of the examples on p. 22 that people find anxiety-creating are 21st century designs, and many, though not all, depend on spaces being controlled electronically and electrically. So it's tempting to think that before the invention of electricity, life might have been easier for people like us who found small spaces difficult. But let's think again. Here's a highly simplified lightning tour of confined spaces through the ages.

BUILDINGS

"Stately homes? Castles? I can't go in them. You never know where the exit is or if they'll take you into cellars or down narrow corridors"

"I had my first claustrophobic attack at the Pyramids. Came out of nowhere. I just had to get out".

"In the spiral staircase of the Leaning Tower of Pisa I suddenly realised that if I wanted to get out, I couldn't. It was really hard not to panic".

Many of today's would-be tourists who experience claustrophobia choose to avoid castles, monasteries, churches and other sites of historical interest for fear of the small and constricted spaces we may encounter. Narrow passageways, tortuous, windowless, spiral stone stairways, endless chambers of underground crypts and catacombs are not fun. Very few of these buildings would conform to modern building safety regulations or provide easy access to exits. Whilst the majority of our ancestors did not live in or even visit such places, and whilst people were generally shorter than today, we can imagine there could well have been those who would have found such buildings anxiety-provoking.

There remain few houses in the UK resembling those still found in rural and village Europe, where interiors are often dark and passageways between houses extremely narrow. Ordinary homes in our villages, towns, and later in cities were frequently small with few windows, built with shelter against the weather as the priority rather than aesthetics. Such restricting conditions would have been compounded for poorer people by the need to share bed space with several siblings!

In the countryside at least people would have spent the majority of their day out-of-doors, in fresh air. But the move to and growth of industrial cities created 'slum' housing of extremely claustrophobic proportions, compounded by the sense of being shut in under overcast, polluted skies, with very little 'leisure' time.

LACK OF LIGHT

At any time in the past when light was removed, anyone with a claustrophobic fear of the dark would have had a problem at night. In WWII, for example, many people hated this aspect of the black-out, and would do anything for a bit of light to ease their panic. At least then it was usually possible to restore light quickly after the "all-clear" siren.

Before the invention of electricity, and before gas lights, the world was dependent on fire, candles and wicks in oil. Without access to a means of lighting a flame, the darkness would have been impenetrable inside buildings. This problem would be compounded for children, for sick people or for prisoners, the latter often held - and possibly forgotten - in windowless underground cells.

As a society, we still use confinement as punishment. We know that it is hard to endure long periods in small spaces. Inmates of all kinds have to manage whatever claustrophobic feelings they encounter in prison, as best they can. We might ask ourselves whether constantly having to cope with claustrophobic feelings creates conditions under which people will, spontaneously, improve their view of society, or their place in it (*see* Addendum p. 262).

SHIPS

Anyone who has visited the Cutty Sark or seen Ridley Scott's powerful film "*Master and Commander*" would remember the extraordinarily claustrophobic atmosphere of life "below deck" in tall ships. So whilst being at sea in an open boat might have its pleasures for some, being press-ganged - forced - into the navy, and compelled to spend many months at sea with little respite, must have created huge claustrophobic fear for others. And even worse, the hideous conditions onboard ships in which slaves were "exported" from Africa must surely have induced claustrophobia. Forced to lie head to toe in tight rows, with only inches of breathing space above the nose, chained in position below deck on a rough ocean, there could be almost nothing so cruel and inhumane.

WORKING ENVIRONMENTS

Throughout the industrial revolution, millions of people were packed into noisy, dirty, dangerous factory environments, working on movement-constraining machinery and monotonous production lines of all kinds. The English writer Thomas Hardy was amongst many observers in protesting against the de-humanising and indeed dangerous conditions workers had to endure.

Whilst the situation may have improved in the West, and whilst most people have been liberated from such a working environment by technology in the switch away from manufacturing towards a service economy, similar constraining conditions are still the norm in many developing countries.

In many mining communities, boys and young men would often have had no alternative to following their fathers into the coal-pits. Without modern ventilation and lift technology, the tunnels and shafts would have been even more suffocating and claustrophobia-inducing than today, compounded by the constant anxiety that an explosion or collapse of supports might bring the primal terror of being buried alive. Despite vastly improved safety procedures, tragically, this can of course still happen. Though fortunately, not always: a collective sigh of profound relief greeted the news recently that thousands of South African miners were rescued unhurt after several days trapped underground.

In our recent history, another group of men has been forced to go underground. During World War II, when miners had been called up to fight, the UK was facing the imminent end of its coal supplies. Fifty thousand men were conscripted to work in mines instead of going into military service (known as 'Bevin Boys' after the Minister of Labour, Ernest Bevin). One of these, Morris Pearce, * really wanted to join the Royal Marines. To try to avoid his mining duty, he claimed to be acutely claustrophobic. Unfortunately for him, when he went to his appeal, there were twenty-four other "acute claustrophobics" present, so - *"this ploy did not work"*. Presumably for some of the twenty-four, claiming claustrophobia was a reality and

* www.newburytoday.co.uk/News.Article.aspx?articleID=4683

not a ploy; we can only hope they were assigned elsewhere. Along with other surviving Bevin Boys, Mr. Pearce will be honoured in 2008 with a 'Badge of Pride', acknowledging the contribution they made.

Earlier, in World War I, British and Allied servicemen had to contend with another claustrophobic situation. Skilled miners created hundreds of miles of cramped tunnels under the battlefields of Northern France and Belgium. Whatever their feelings, soldiers would have had to have found the courage to use these, as they formed essential lines of communication and surprise attack. Trench warfare was devastating enough; the very real possibility of being trapped underground must have compounded the wretchedness of the situation.

BEING BURIED ALIVE

The fear of being buried alive is deep-seated. Before the invention of sophisticated emergency machinery for locating and rescuing people from landslides, avalanches, typhoons, earthquake rubble, mining disasters and bomb damage, the probability of emerging alive was far slimmer.

Fear of accidental burial on the basis of misdiagnosis of death in the nineteenth century led to the formation of the *Society for the Prevention of People Being Buried Alive*. Coffins could be fitted with complicated emergency equipment to be used if someone woke to found him or herself buried (such devices continued to be invented to as recently as 1995). Some even went so far as to specify in their wills that their throats should be cut (to make sure they were really *really* dead) before burial. There was limited evidence (of premature burial) on which this fear could be based, although there were some few recorded instances during times of plague, for example. But like many other fears, this anxiety about an extremely rare possibility could reach phobic proportions.

Such a fear is still with us, despite the advances of modern medicine.

Some of the people who have shared their anxieties with me spontaneously mentioned this fear – and usually switched the conversation away from the thought immediately, with a shudder. It's unbearable. It's unthinkable. (Thirty years ago I had a pact with a friend that if either of us died, the other would secretly give us a good poke with something sharp (we decided on knitting needles) - just to be sure. And somewhere in my psyche I know there is still the hope that she'd give it a go … The recent controversy about the creation of 'living wills' may be a related phenomenon: determining in advance that we would not wish to be 'trapped' inside our own bodies).

OTHER TIMES, OTHER ENCLOSED SPACES

There are many other situations which continue into the present but were likely worse in the past. Queuing, for example, cited by many as inducing claustrophobic feelings, is hardly a new phenomenon. Where the queue was for hand-to-mouth work at the docks, factories and building sites, or for rationed food, the desperately essential nature of what was being queued for surely made queuing harder than waiting to hear when our planes will leave for holiday destinations, or sitting on a motorway: (in Whitstable, in Kent, the place where men queued for work in the oyster fisheries was known as Starvation Point, not without reason).

In other areas of life, safety regulations in public buildings, factories and music halls were limited and exits frequently inaccessible or inappropriately few in number, leading to infamous disasters. Into the 1800's you could still be imprisoned for stealing a loaf; convicts were shackled in irons whilst being transported, years after slavery ended. Patients in asylums were imprisoned in strait-jackets. Masks, detested by many, were forcibly held over the face to give anaesthetic gas for operations. Diving masks were monstrous objects, screwed into position and impossible to remove by oneself. Smoking was permitted in the London underground until as late as 1987.

So this highly condensed overview of life before the electronic age suggests that it was far from being a claustrophobia-free Arcadia. In fact, conditions in many walks of life could be considered far better now than they have ever been.

Does this then lead us to draw the conclusion that to experience claustrophobia now is completely irrational? That those of us who experience claustrophobia should just "*feel the fear and do it anyway*", "*get a grip*", "*manage our moods*" and discount our fears as meaningless and having no substance?

I don't think so. I accept that a phobic reaction can be over-blown - all of us who experience claustrophobia recognise this, when we are able to engage our rational minds, when we are not gripped with panic. And we often get to the point of wanting to get the better of it, to help ourselves and the people who have supported us.

But to make headway with overcoming our fears, we really need to know whether there is any basis for our fear, however slim. Profound changes have occurred in the way we live and in the development and use of technology, creating new forms of confinement. I believe there to be a kernel of truth in our claustrophobic fears that is a profoundly human rejection of being enclosed and confined, especially by impersonal electronic means.

To blindly dismiss our own or someone else's fears as wholly "phobic" is to discount our recognition of the traumatic effects, and sometimes the danger, however slight, of such enclosure.

And without objection, without reflection, without care, these changes will continue inexorably, and we will find ourselves further confined in ways we cannot control. This truth needs expression to those who have influence over the structure of every aspect of our environment: *"faceless authorities, whether they be utility companies or chains"*, as the commentator Stephen Bayley has described them. And those of us who experience claustrophobia can help.

Contributor responses to electronically controlled space

"I have recently learned that London taxicab doors are locked while the vehicle is in transit, so they too are now unavailable to me unless I can first check that the window will open far enough to allow an awfully improbable escape. This new fear illustrates, I think, the irrationality of it all. I could never be tempted to jump from a moving vehicle but I have to know that is possible"

"I can't go on long journeys by train anymore because of the electronic push button automatic doors, which are horrendous"

"I got locked in my car when the key battery was flat. I couldn't get out, and I freaked out completely. Couldn't connect to anything or understand what was going

on. I tried the doors and windows and I couldn't make anything work. Finally I managed to telephone my husband on my mobile, and he calmed me down enough to try all the doors; eventually I found one at the back that opened. It was totally terrifying. I had no idea those keys could go flat like that. I think it's incredibly dangerous. What if the car had gone into water?"

"We were in a hovercraft, sealed in on a very stormy sea, and a huge wave came over the ship. I was sobbing and clinging to the steward, a total stranger".

"I got stuck on a crowded train from Glasgow for more than an hour, in a ten hour journey: the crew got off the train, the heating was left on, there was no information, no water, no windows that could be opened. I had to leave the children and go to first class where it was cooler. Someone took charge and took me there, and I had to leave the children with a kind woman who offered to help. There was no point in feeling guilty. I felt torn between my real panic and my strong instinct to take care of the children. It was very difficult".

"My friend got stuck in her house when there was a power-cut. She was frightened - she had had no idea that the security gates wouldn't work without electricity. I think it's dangerous"

"I can't repeat the journey (on a crowded line), especially since the arrival of Virgin's tilting trains, with no window that passengers can open"

"There seem to be so many more claustrophobic situations now. Trains with automatic doors, ferries with no outer deck, rooms with low ceilings and no windows, buses with less seats to allow more people to crowd in together"

"It takes a fifteen mg dose of Valium to persuade me to lock the door in those tiny airborne lavatories. But worse, these days, are the loos on trains, where you need to identify a letter or number code on a keyboard pad before the door will open and let you out"

"New style transport systems with automatic doors may be 'safer' in some ways but are not helpful to those with claustrophobia"

"It really frightens me to think how unsafe such journeys are, with apparently unlimited numbers of people allowed to travel on a train"

KEY CHANGES THAT MAY BE CREATING MORE CLAUSTROPHOBIC CONDITIONS

"Putting hominoids into close proximity and inviting them to engage in serial acts of competitive individualism could not be considered a good idea. You put rats in claustrophobic circumstances and they become ... murderous and cannibalistic in no time at all".
Stephen Bayley in reviewing
'Cities for a Small Planet', by Richard Rogers,
for The Independent, London, 1997

Having our space or freedom of movement restricted, feeling out of control, or feeling cut off from people we know, can all be triggers to claustrophobia. The following changes in the way we live together suggest that such factors are likely to increase.

1   Urban drift and time indoors

Our population increasingly lives in cities and urbanised areas, a phenomenal drift - or indeed, rush away from the land. The vast majority of us spend the greater part of the day inside buildings, in contrast with earlier generations, most of whom would have regarded houses as shelter, spending most daylight hours outside. This is a massive shift over the last two hundred years, in evolutionary terms, and there is no reason to suppose that as animals, we have all completely adapted physically and neurologically to our 'new' circumstances of daily confinement.

2   Crowding, heterogeneity and individual expression

Towns, cities, roads and trains have and will become increasingly crowded, with greater competition for space, contributing to the feeling of claustrophobia (and we're all becoming larger! - so less of us can fit into the same space as we used to). Successfully dealing with high density living, working and travelling, without becoming highly stressed, requires respect and restraint. If you consider yourself a small part of the collective '*we*', it may be easier to cope with confined and crowded spaces than where the emphasis is on '*I*'.

In Japan, until relatively recently, a common value system, the mores of self-discipline, controlled movement, and highly structured patterns of courtesy were all greatly revered within the exceedingly homogenous population. Such behaviour enabled vast numbers of people to live, work and travel together in extremely close proximity on the narrow strips of habitable land. This is, after all, the land of the bonsai tree and the capsule hotel - as well as a subway system that defies the imagination in terms of numbers of people carried each day.

In our heterogeneous society, there is historically a far greater attachment to individual expression. We believe in others' rights to the same freedoms, although we know these may conflict. As Britain becomes increasingly crowded, the diversity of the population is also widening, with a commensurate diversification of individual values, priorities, expectations and needs. Inevitably, there will be incompatibility in how these values and needs will be expressed, and how resources, including space, should be used, and by whom.

3   Expectations of freedom

In the last sixty years, we have learnt to expect to be ultra-mobile, to control how and where we want to go, to get what we need and want by 'going for it'. Increasingly, we expect life - including all things electronic - to work, never to break down, to progress, to move and to move fast - at the speed of thought, or at the speed of broadband (whichever is the faster). If we are not being productive, creative, dynamic and involved, we wonder what we're being, or even *if* we are being. We are encouraged to believe our choices should be unlimited, and that all our potential should be realised: that every obstacle is removable, if we 'dig deep enough', if we truly believe *'we're worth it'*. At every level, actual and metaphorical, *we simply do not expect to be confined.*

Being still, waiting, doing nothing and staring into space seems to hold relatively little value. So we don't enter confined spaces slowly, with an expectation of dawdling in there. We expect to move in and move out immediately. We may dissociate to endure being pressed up against humanity, but if the train doors don't open the second we press the button, how quickly we find ourselves jabbing it again and again. How many of us see a traffic jam and immediately try to think of an alternative route, however far out of our way it may take us? Anything rather than being 'forced' to stay still for a while (even if that could give us an opportunity to relax).

So when we are confined, or if we imagine we're going to be trapped, it's as if all the after-images of our perpetual forward-moving individualism have nowhere to go but into us, creating a turmoil of frustration, rage, confusion. Anxiety builds. What are we to do with the thrust of our onward-going engines if our flightpath is blocked? Witness 'road rage', where simple driving mistakes can have people snarling and swearing at each other within a moment. It's rare that the anger was created by the actual situation, it's simply being expressed there. If we are 'supposed' to be in control, who wouldn't avoid a repeat of this situation?

Despite the Slow Movement, or major oil shortages, it's hard to envisage what might create the circumstances for anything less than an acceleration of the tempo of living, or a growth in our demand to move freely, directly conflicting with our demands for safety.

4   Increasing fear of attack, and the drive towards security

At the same time, our demands for security are increasing, or are being imposed on us by governments intent on keeping us safe from the reality or possibility of crime or terrorist threat. We British are watched and hemmed around by more cameras than any other population in the world. We believe that crime is increasing, even when research indicates that it is not, and we look for systems that keep all danger at bay, and other people with dubious intentions, out. We increasingly rely on electronic systems to identify us and judge whether we are acceptable or not. In the process, we effectively lock ourselves up in our homes, cars, gated communities and offices, behind laminated, unbreakable glass and solid doors.

Electronic systems can protect, but they can equally marginalise and exclude.

I once witnessed a scene in a small village in southern France where an elderly man was trapped in the air-lock style entrance of his bank because the electronic system interpreted his metal hip as a weapon. Whatever system the bank brought in to protect its staff and customers should have been conceived in such a way as to prioritise and include him, not exclude or inconvenience. When Monsieur le War Hero, who lost his leg defending La Liberté (as he told the whole village), is effectively held captive by a bank he has used for decades, something has gone very wrong in the balance between security and freedom. An over-emphasis on protection reduces human contact: makes being known, being recognised, having our needs and personal interest considered, all those things that make any service worth using, or life worth living, of lesser importance. Such an imbalance can lead to an increase in confined spaces, and a potential for the kinds of trauma that can kick-start claustrophobia.

5   Electronically controlled space

Our use of spaces *enclosed by means beyond our control* has changed massively since the advent of electrical and electronic technology. Even up to the 1950's in the UK, the vast majority of the working population walked to work, or caught an open-doored bus or a train with windows and doors that could be opened by hand. Many living outside cities would never have needed to use lifts in their day-to-day lives. High-rise buildings that depended on lifts to reach homes and offices on the top floors were still relatively rare outside cities. Most people had never flown. Doors - to buildings and vehicles everywhere - opened mechanically, and were locked with solid metal keys.

Contrast this with our society where huge numbers of

working people commute, which increasingly means travelling on trains, buses, tube trains, cars and taxis with electronically sealed doors (and in many cases windows as well). A large section of the population flies, and flies more often.   Many people have to take lifts to get to their work place or even go to and from their own front doors. Many houses and flats are enclosed behind electronically controlled security gates; there is even 'central locking' available for houses. The doors to hotel rooms are increasingly operated electronically, and have sealed, double glazed widows of unbreakable glass. Doors and lifts operated by electronic fingerprint recognition and voice recognition are increasingly common, no longer limited to specialist facilities.   *More people have to allow themselves to be impersonally confined than ever before.*

Why should any of this be a problem? If there is a power-cut, the electronic gates of your house will not necessarily open; you are shut in, and the ambulance trying to reach you is shut out. If your speeding train is involved in an accident, you may find it a great deal harder to leave the carriage than you would if you could climb through a window. If the lift does not recognise your voice, or fails to take that paper-cut on your finger into account, how will it know when you want to get out? If the computer tells the authority that you are Mr. X. when you are in fact Mr. Y - (as a German friend of ours experienced on presenting his ID card) - how will you prove that you are who you say you are?

In the past, the means to escape from enclosed circumstances was largely dependent on physical strength, a knowledge of how things worked, and relationships. The more impervious the structures we build, the more the kind of strength required to escape becomes super-human. But our population is aging, and there will be more of us with reduced strength and mobility. As technology has developed, the gap between what an ordinary person knows and what the designer of a car, train, plane, lift or electronically operated door knows, is increasingly vast.

6   Alienation

The more anonymous and impersonal our society becomes, compounded by the distancing of computer verified identify, the less likely we are to be known as individuals. When lives were more predictable, families and communities closer, less transitory and more settled, we could trust that someone somewhere would probably miss us if we were separated and trapped. Clearly there are exceptions to this – soldiers and sailors travelling overseas for years were not named individually to the nation if they lost their lives. But if you lived in a mining community, and there was a disaster at the pit, every man would be accounted for, every wife at the colliery gate would know exactly who went in and who came out. In World War II, there was huge confidence that neighbours and friends as well as the official wardens and rescue teams would search for people who were buried during bombing.

There is evidence from recent disasters to suggest that in large incidents of all kinds, the public at large can behave with generosity and courage in trying to help each other, especially if they feel the place they call 'home' is under attack. However, there is equally no doubt that there are many instances of mass panic in the instinctual flight for self-preservation, and that we are all likely to prioritise those dearest to us, rather than strangers.

Which will prevail, as more of us live alone than ever before, less involved with our communities, more likely to be living amongst unknown strangers than in close-knit networks of family and friends? Could some part of our claustrophobia reflect our fears of, or indeed actual experience of, increasing alienation and isolation?

Chapter 6

Canaries in the coalmine?
Claustrophobia and inclusive design

The fear of small and confined spaces is a deeply human response to the possibility of being trapped. This fear has stayed with us as we evolved out of caves (hopefully high ceiling-ed and roomy ones) into hi-tech 21st century living. Most human responses that endure through the great march of history have a survival value. So there is every reason to imagine that claustrophobia serves a similar protective purpose for our species.

I believe that those of us who experience claustrophobia can make a genuine contribution to improving the environment for everyone. Our sensitivity to the dangers and discomforts of being enclosed can remind everyone involved in the design and construction of any space that holds humans, be it a building, a form of transport, or a kind of medical equipment, of the importance of recognising and prioritising the human dimension.

We're not isolated atoms spinning in space, we're part of the world community. The philosopher Heidegger suggests that our personal feelings *disclose* something about society as a whole. We don't need to view our claustrophobia as an individual malaise, or a fault in us. If we have these feelings, then so do others, in more ways than we can imagine. Once we can discriminate between valid concern about potential dangers or discomfort, and the effects of our fear of fear, and manage that, then we can use our environmental sensitivity and imagination to call for improvement.

In this way, our role may be similar to that of the canaries which were taken down coal mines even as late as the 1990's.

Deep underground, ventilation was difficult and supplies of clean air essential. The miners were in constant danger of a build-up of methane and carbon monoxide, which could result in poisoned air or an explosion. Canaries are highly sensitive to these gases. If there were even small quantities present in the air, the little yellow birds would begin to sway or stop singing, and become visibly distressed. At a higher concentration of poisonous gas, the birds would simply fall unconscious and die.

So the miners would receive an early warning, and they could immediately leave the mine before they too became unconscious, or there was an explosion. Did they take their life-saving canaries with them? (it's the first question anyone with a hint of claustrophobia - or even compassion - asks). C.J. R. Kitchen, Secretary of the National Union of Mineworkers, assured me they did.

When people who experience claustrophobia '*stop singing*', and even more so when we become '*visibly distressed*', perhaps it is also a warning. A warning that when society focuses on the demands of technology, is captivated by ever greater speed, becomes mesmerised by the wonders of electronically controlled systems, or disproportionately prioritises security over freedom of movement, it may lose sight of what real flesh-and-blood people actually want, need, or find tolerable and enjoyable.

Let's look at two classic examples from two different centuries. The first comes from the building of the underground system in London. The advent of electric trains enabled engineers to lay track and build tunnels deep under London for the first time (previous tubes trains had been steam driven, with tracks laid much closer to the surface). One of these deep lines was the South and Central Line, which no longer exists. There were three design elements in these new trains that make modern tube travel seem like heaven by comparison.

Firstly, the doors on the carriages could only be opened from the outside, so 'gatemen' had to be positioned on the underground platforms at intervals, to let the passengers out. Secondly, because electricity was new, there were regular power failures, which meant that people would often be stuck underground, between stations, in the pitch darkness. And lastly, almost unbelievably, the designers didn't bother to put any windows in the carriages, because *'there was nothing for the passengers to see'*. Needless to say, despite the speed this new system offered (when it worked), the trains were not at all popular, and design improved.

The second example is more recent. The first MRI scanners (magnetic resonance imaging) were clearly built with the new technology in mind, rather than the feelings of the humans they were designed to help. Early scanners were built as narrow tubes, with a bore not much more greater than a human body, closed at one end, and often built into walls - in one case, in London, in a crypt! According to Vikki Ayton, the Director of Operations at the Upright MRI Centre in London, they were extremely noisy, and badly lit. Patients were strapped onto a conveyor belt to go into the scanner, often head-first (even for scans that did not involve the head), and were required to lie absolutely still for extended periods, unable to see out.

Research not only shows that between five and fifteen percent of patients refused to complete the procedure, with a further thirty percent finding the experience very unpleasant, but also that *claustrophobia was actually triggered for some people for the first time,* a traumatic result of going through this procedure. Regrettably, on occasion, the stress of the situation was compounded by insensitivity from staff, reported to have described distressed patients as being *'awkward'* or *'difficult customers'*, and treating anxiety and panic dismissively.

When a patient cannot bring him or herself to go through an MRI scan, or stay there long enough for useable scans to be taken, then valuable (and expensive) scanner and staff time is lost. The patient's condition, which initially brought him into contact with medical services, will require other, potentially less effective means of investigation, and there could be further delay in diagnosis.

Fortunately, staff and designers have recognised that it isn't the apprehensive patient who is the problem, but rather the constraints of the procedure. Not only have conventional scanners been hugely updated and improved (opened at both ends, the bore widened, mirrors fitted to enable the patient to see staff, noise reduced and so on) but two completely different designs of MRI have been developed. One is open, in two halves like a hamburger (in which the patient is a rather inelegant, but hopefully relaxed, filling). The other is upright: not only can you sit or stand, but you can also watch DVDs and see friends nearby in the scanner suite, much like sitting on a bicycle.

I see these new scanners as representing a triumph of human sensibility over the 'demands' of technology (albeit helpful technology). They restore dignity, respect and control to the patient (*for more on scanners, see* p. 180).

Improvement in scanner design was driven at least in part by the need to lower the 'refusal' rate of claustrophobic patients. The provision of windows and proper doors on tube carriages was presumably driven by the need to provide return to the original investors in the South and Central line, by encouraging more people to travel. But these design improvements have benefited everyone, whether they think of themselves as claustrophobic or not. Both experiences have become far less stressful for all concerned.

These two examples fulfil many of the key principles of

'inclusive design', as described by the Commission for Architecture and the Built Environment. The CABE is the UK government's advisor on architecture, urban design and public space, aiming to encourage policy makers to create welcoming places that work for people, and to inspire the public to demand more from our buildings and spaces.

According to CABE, in the world of buildings, inclusive design (also known as *design for all* and *universal design*) puts people at the heart of the design process, promoting well-being and social cohesion. It acknowledges diversity and difference, and doesn't create 'disabling barriers' for particular members of the public. It acknowledges that access isn't just about the physical lay-out of a building; it's also about 'intellectual' and 'emotional' aspects that people need to feel confident about before using the space. Inclusive design offers choice, and recognises that if the needs of a diverse population are taken on board, then what CABE calls 'superior solutions' will be found that actually benefit everyone. Inclusive design provides flexibility in how facilities are used, and creates environments that are comfortable and enjoyable for everyone.

Whilst CABE focuses on buildings and space, the Helen Hamlyn Research Centre at the Royal College of Arts stresses that principles of inclusive design should be observed by designers of all products and services. This surely includes any space that holds humans.

So through the justifiable protests of people who experience claustrophobia, and the designers who took note of them, 'superior solutions' were found in the two unrelated fields of underground travel and MRI scanners, making them both genuinely safer, more comfortable, and more accessible; less likely to trigger claustrophobia. And no doubt there is a lot more development that could improve both services further, in line with inclusive design thinking.

That doesn't mean that design solutions have to be a dull '*one size fits all*', or be reduced to the lowest common denominator. Vincent Kirk, for example, from KkeArchitects*, designs hospice accommodation providing terminally-ill patients with windows in their rooms at bed height, so that they can see out to landscaped gardens designed to attract wildlife. Such innovation could be seen as excluding upright staff and relatives (for whom full height windows are provided), but certainly do a lot for the patient.

The windows extend the dimensions of the room outwards, reducing the feeling of being confined and trapped. They give a view of nature, with positive implications for reduced stress and increased interest in life (*see* p. 113 *on the benefits of the natural environment*). But just as importantly, they give unwell patients a capacity that the healthy staff don't have (or need so much). The patient's sense of retaining a unique view on the world is increased, making them less dependent on staff, for example for weather reports, or for fresh things to talk about. Such a patient is likely to be calmer, more interested, more relaxed, which must surely benefit both their well-being and the staff caring for them. This kind of imaginative, lateral thinking about confined space benefits everyone. But it needs to be extended to all kinds of architecture not only in medical facilities.

Finally, let's look at two other situations that people who experience claustrophobia find difficult - one perhaps more a matter of 'inconvenience', the other, a genuine potential danger – where advances in design have resolved some problems, been inclusive, only to create new issues, and potential exclusion.

Loos are no doubt a minor detail for most architects and

* *see* Resources

designers, and yet stress stirred up by poor design could so easily be avoided with a little thought. The advent of electronically controlled toilet facilities is not universally welcomed. This is a compilation of ideas from contributors to this book, on what would make loos so much easier to manage …

PEOPLE WHO EXPERIENCE CLAUSTROPHOBIA WOULD PREFER -

✔ loos that were not miles away from civilisation at the back of basements, down long empty corridors or tucked under stairs

✔ the top of the door or sides of cubicles to be open, even if only by a small way, or even better, partition loos where doors and walls are just deep enough to satisfy modesty!

✔ the lock to simply slide into a bar on the inside of the doorframe, rather than burying itself inside the frame, which means there is no way of getting out if it gets stuck

✔ mirrors, which make even the tiniest loo look bigger

✔ loos on trains that could still be opened, locked and unlocked manually

✔ the removal and replacement of all electronically-controlled public loos!

Whence came the demand for the loos on trains which *excluded* mechanical escape? Bigger space, yes, to allow for wheelchairs: easier access to controls, yes. But with no alternative mechanical system to unlock or open the door, many people feel too vulnerable to use them, and either can't take long journeys or only do so in a state of anxiety and discomfort.

The second example concerns design advances in cars. People who experience claustrophobia frequently have concerns about travelling in cars with central locking systems, with no windows that can be opened manually. Such anxiety, about how escape could be managed in the event of an accident, is not wholly irrational. In 2003 the Dutch Transport Safety Board conducted a safety study into the problem of escaping from cars submerged in water (*see* Resources). They discovered that most people lacked basic information on what to do on the rare occasions this happened, but more importantly, that many people didn't know which window would be easiest to break for escape under *any* emergency circumstances*.

Despite the advantages of greater driver safety and resistance to break-in, the report describes advances in car technology (stronger bonded and electrically operated windows, anti-theft systems and comfort locking) as creating vehicles that are like *'impregnable fortresses'* (p.23 of the report) making both escape, and access to occupants, increasingly difficult in case of accident. The report notes that some user manuals actually state that '*driving with centrally locked doors can hinder outside assistance in the event of an emergency'* (p.24, ibid).

Their recommendations included having additional questions on escape information in the driving test: lobbying for Dutch passenger cars and government vehicles to be equipped with easy-to-reach 'life hammers', and that if research on existing hammers showed they were not capable of smashing the new, stronger, windows, then *'insofar as and as long as no adequate solutions is (sic) found, consumers need to be warned of the dangers'* (p.28, ibid).

The dangers of driving into water in the UK are slimmer than in the Netherlands, but our cars are developing in the same direction.

---

* *for guidelines from the Dutch Institute for Road Safety Research, see* Resources

Manually open-able widows are becoming a thing of the past. At the time of writing (2007), *questions on how to escape from cars are not included in the UK driving test.* No legislation exists or is proposed to have cars fitted with 'life hammers'.

The solution designed to deal with one safety issue has created a new problem. 'Superior solutions' need to deal with both.

Many people who experience claustrophobia feel that they have no right to express dissatisfaction or concern about the confined spaces they find difficult, or sense as actually dangerous, as this typical comment from one of the contributors shows:

> *"I have never thought of voicing my opinion, because I always assumed I was the problem".*

We do have a 'right'. Because if we find the dimensions, structure or design of a space anxiety-provoking, we can be sure that we are not alone - many other people will too. There may well be a rationale for our disquiet. Sometimes we can draw attention to a situation which might have traumatised or been dangerous for someone else: as the patients who expressed dislike of the MRI scans did, the would-be underground travellers did, as passenger groups did who called for more accessible window exits on trains after the Paddington Rail crash, as the Dutch transport authorities have. Our fears of small spaces should not be pathologised into purely a 'mental health disorder' or some personal weakness. Beneath our heightened and sometimes inappropriate assessment of danger, there may be absolutely valid concerns.

So we can protest when we're herded into over-full trains or told that we shouldn't expect to be able to sit down on journeys of thirty minutes or less. We can resist being pressed into packed lifts at the airport and demand we be allowed to use escalators and stairs. We can support car companies that make models with windows that can be opened manually, that provide keys that can be operated mechanically. We can complain when ferry companies make passengers wait on crewless car decks. We can tell department stores that there is a shortage of exit signs, and hospitals that their mirror-less lifts and bleak corridors are alienating. We can suggest to transport companies there should be protocols for how often drivers speak to passengers, and when.

If we think about what could be done to improve the situation, if we speak out, then the possibilities for a better, safer, more comfortable environment for everyone, expand.

Of course, we can't ask for guarantees. Accidents and incidents happen, people get hurt. And if we want to fly, we have to leave the ground, and there's no point asking for a window to open. If we want to travel very quickly to France, we have to accept that the train will go underground and under water. Not every sound the aircraft or train or lift makes indicates imminent catastrophe. Not every failure of a lift or train door opening means we will be stuck forever and ever. And the vast majority of people are benevolent, or indifferent, to their fellow passengers, and are not out to hurt us.

The more those of us who experience claustrophobia learn to distinguish between our 'phobic' response and our valid anxieties, we better we can draw attention to enclosed spaces which are either genuinely dangerous, or are potentially traumatising for us and for other people. In this way, we can contribute to the creation of a safer, more open, more pleasurable environment for everyone.

And as human canaries, we can keep singing.

Part 3
Finding your way out

Chapter 7

What helps?
An overview

Why do you want to overcome claustrophobia? This may sound like a strange question, but it will help if you can clarify your personal motivation. When the going gets tough, remembering your motivation will help you persist. Try framing your statement positively: So - could it be

> Because I want to feel free to do what I need and want to
> do, without massive anxiety
>
> Because I want to know I can soothe my anxieties, or
> tolerate them
>
> Because I want to go back to my job
>
> *or*
>
> Because I want to be able to change jobs
>
> Because I want to be able to see all the members of my
> family and friends, no matter where they live
>
> Because I want my children to have a role-model for
> overcoming anxiety, not being crushed by it
>
> Because …???

And how will we know if we have overcome or recovered from claustrophobia?

We don't have to be able to go into the furthest depths of a deep-sea mine, or to the moon in a space capsule, to 'prove' our phobia is defeated. Nor is it realistic to set ourselves up to believe that 'success' or 'recovery' means we can now guarantee that confined spaces will never again make us feel frightened, under any circumstances.

Firstly, we don't have to prove anything, to anyone. Our own success can be much more modest and subtle. It's about knowing we can reduce our 'fear about fear', as much as feeling confident we'll be able to cope with the fear itself. It might simply be using taxis, trains and buses like you used to. Having the confidence to use any loo or any lift or tunnel you might encounter if you visited friends or went on holiday: shopping anywhere you want: going into your bank through the security lock or revolving door. Or flying, without spending entire long-haul flights with your fingers (or indeed legs!) crossed. It might be a minor aspect of life, or it might be fundamental, like being able to return to the job you love, or look for a new job without feeling terrified at the prospect of new journeys and workplaces (*have a look at the list on p. 22 to help you decide what your top five targets might be*).

Secondly, as I've mentioned throughout this book, aiming to totally eradicate fear is not the point. We need fear, and all its accompanying physiological changes, to keep us alert to the dangers in our world and to mobilise us to take appropriate action. Thirdly, none of us can ever entirely know what might make us frightened, or what accidents or incidents will occur in our lives. We can't ask for absolute guarantees of perfect safety. Or we can ask, but sadly, we probably won't get.

'Recovery' from claustrophobia is about feeling free and confident *to do what we want to do and go where we want to go*, no longer avoiding the possibility of feeling fear or dealing with genuine threat in the confined spaces we might encounter. It's knowing that we will have a far greater chance to hold onto our stability, thinking and sense of well-being in the face of threat, than we did when fear kept us away.

So the bottom line is that we each have a choice. If claustrophobia keeps our lives smaller than they need be, by preventing us doing things or going to places that might be frightening, do we want to exist within those limitations, or do we want to expand and push them back - make more space for ourselves?

It's a profound decision - and a paradoxical one. It means deciding to risk moving beyond the restrictions created by our fear, by choosing to go into or through the confined places and spaces we've avoided.

Once you've decided that you want to deal with your claustrophobia, various alternatives present themselves. What helps? We'll all have individual answers. In the next section you'll find suggestions from a wide range of sources that have helped both the contributors and myself. Whatever alternative you choose, *the proof of the pudding is in the eating*, so the key question has to be: *Is this alternative you've chosen helping you to use or go through the confined spaces you were avoiding?*

The only way to find out if your choice is working for you is to go back into the confined spaces and find out. There's a lot in here about trust. Trust that we will look after ourselves, that we'll do our best to cope with whatever we experience. Trust that we won't abandon ourselves when the going gets tough. And trust that other people wish us well, both friends and strangers, and that they will probably want to offer help when we need it. *The more we feel connected to the other people in our lives, the more whatever strategy we choose will help us.*

Whatever choice of strategy you make, whether it be learning to self-soothe, a gradual increase in your tolerance of anxiety, some support from a therapist or buddy, or many more lateral and creative techniques, it's worth equipping yourself with new resources before you try your first experiment. It's important to know that you can start changing your experience for the better, at any moment, and at every moment. It's important to know you have choice. Developing our deepest, wisest selves can help us make those changes and choices well.

Developing a benign internal witness or 'wise self'

"When I get claustrophobic, I can't think straight anymore. My brain is scrambled. The only thing that's going on inside me is an animal feeling of I HAVE TO GET OUT!"

Part of the common and disabling experience for people who have claustrophobia is of being overwhelmed by a flood of panic and terror, and at the same time, in that moment of feeling or being trapped, not being able to think. It's what leads to mass panics, which have often been averted when even one person has managed to *"... keep their head when all about (them) are losing theirs ..."*
Not being able to think can be truly terrifying, hard perhaps for anyone to imagine if they have not had that experience. We have to be able to think to look after ourselves as well as others, and to manage the situation we find ourselves in. And *believing that you will not be able to think* is, for an adult, a frightening prospect in itself. It's unlikely that many people would put themselves into a vulnerable situation, if they thought they would not have tools and strategies for problem-solving their way out, if necessary. Enclosed situations make us feel this vulnerability. So we avoid the possibility of being traumatised again.
Now let's look at another comment from someone who *doesn't* experience claustrophobia or other states of anxiety. Such

a person doesn't want to be rude, but it's obvious they feel baffled, and sometimes even impatient.

> *"I'm sure this sounds very cruel, and I'd never say this to someone who was clearly suffering. But ... isn't it just a question of telling yourself to pull yourself together?"*

This comment is clearly based on the common understanding that we all talk to ourselves, that we have different 'parts' with different aims. Many of us do this a lot *("I really should get out of bed". "Mm, but I'd really like a bit longer, I'm so comfortable" "Oh OK then, but just another five minutes").* One part - a more logical, thinking, organised, knowing, perhaps more authoritative part, can tell another part of the self what to do. It needs the second part to co-operate. There's the sense that the second part of the self is not so organised as the first, and is the one feeling the anxiety. So for our person who is baffled about other people's anxiety, the comment *"Couldn't you just tell yourself to pull yourself together?"* is based on the belief that the feeling part will do what it's told by the thinking part, and that then all will be well.

In moments of sheer panic, people who feel claustrophobic seem to have three common experiences. The first is when *"I tell my 'Self'"* to calm down, or *to "Pull yourself together"* - nothing happens. We can pull all we want, and boy, do we try, but our feeling selves either can't or won't do what he or she is told. Or possibly, 'they' are so busy feeling anxious they don't even hear the instruction, or they feel it is too dangerous to comply. Thirdly, the anxiety may be so overwhelming that we don't feel as if the thinking self is saying anything intelligible at all. *The bottom line is that logic and feelings don't 'speak the same language', and when times get tough, the need for an interpreter is enormous.*

So whatever self-help strategy we undertake, whatever therapy we go to, the key thing we can do for ourselves as people who experience claustrophobia is to *strengthen the loving and constructive connection between the different parts of ourselves*, between 'I' and my 'Self', between our thinking and feeling selves. To do this, we need to develop a third aspect of ourselves, our internal witness, interpreter or mediator, who can listen to *'the other two'* and help them develop mutual respect and understanding. Our wise self needs to be able to 'speak' in a voice that can reach and connect with our emotions and our thoughts, within the safe home of our bodies.

Without that respect and connection, we won't trust our powers of risk assessment, or allow ourselves to be soothed. We won't allow the thought that people care about us to calm us down, and we won't believe our rational side when it says that a thumping heart is not a sign that we're about to have a cardiac arrest. We won't even be able to remind ourselves that we previously stayed in a confined space in our 'hierarchy of fear' to the point where our anxiety dropped. So the experience will be blanked out, and we'll feel as if we're back to square one.

(continues…)

Our 'wise self' needs to choose action in the real world that

- ✔ deepens our self-trust and confidence in our reliability all the time, not just in confined spaces
- ✔ neither discounts risks, nor over-estimates them
- ✔ neither discounts our own abilities, nor over-estimates our confidence or the level of stress we can reasonably handle
- ✔ prioritises increasing self-care and self-respect
- ✔ builds our ability to support ourselves, and allows us to reach out to other people who can support us as well
- ✔ frees us to live in the moment, responding to what is actually happening right here, and right now

In this way, handling claustrophobia becomes just another part of developing ourselves as fully-rounded, resilient human beings, acting from what Bruno Bettelheim described as our *'informed hearts'* - the ability to bring both our hearts and minds to bear on whatever challenges come our way.

Whichever alternative route you choose to take to deal with your claustrophobia, there are many different strategies available.

CHOOSING YOUR WAY FORWARD

I	Do you want to try a *self-help route?*

You'll find lots of strategies throughout the remainder of this book! Some are drawn from the theories underpinning the therapies listed below, and some are other ways of dealing with claustrophobia that have worked for contributors to the book, for me, and for other people (*see* p. 108)

You might also like to learn about the National Phobics' Society, which regularly features a wealth of information about new approaches in its members' newsletters, and offers a range of low cost therapies. Membership also gives the possibility of learning what works for other people (*see* Resources)

2	Do you think or know that your claustrophobia was caused by *a specific trauma,* and that you might need help with that first?

You might want to try Hypnotherapy (p. 230), Eye Movement Desentization & Reprocessing (EMDR) (p. 228), Emotional Freedom Techniques (EFT) (p. 223) or Thought Field Therapy (TFT) (p. 243)

If you may think you may be suffering from Post-Traumatic Stress Disorder *(for symptoms please see Appendix B), be aware that many experts consider deliberate exposure to fear-triggers needs to handled very slowly and gently, so please care for yourself accordingly and seek specific professional support.*

3	Do you want to *suppress or relieve the symptoms* of claustrophobia quickly, in the short term?

You might want to ask your GP for medication (p. 233)

You might want to try a Rescue Remedy (p. 233)

4	Do you want to try the *"getting back on the horse"* method, and face your fears directly, in a confined space, with support?

You might want to try Exposure/desensitization therapy (p. 225) (*and see* CBT, below)

5	Do you have the sense that the *way you are thinking about confined spaces* is part of your problem? Would it be helpful if a professional therapist accompanied you whilst you face some of the situations you fear?

You might want to try Cognitive Behaviour Therapy (CBT) (p. 204)

6	Would you like to *work out your own solutions and strategies,* with some support?
	You might want to try Solution Focused Brief Therapy (p. 242)
	You might want to try Computer-assisted therapy (p. 219)

7	Do you have the sense that your symptoms of claustrophobia might have a *deeper meaning* for you, and you'd like some insight about what might be going on?
	You might want to try - Psychodyamic psychotherapy (p. 233) or Re-birthing therapy (p. 240)

Chapter 8

Self-help strategies

If you decide to use self-help strategies to overcome your claustrophobia, please think about self-care, as well. This might mean checking out with your GP that you don't have any underlying physical health problems or getting support from friends, family or colleagues. *Most importantly, I believe it means not putting yourself in situations that are irreversible until you have built up your confidence in coping with situations where escape is easy.* There is no one perfect strategy or method that will suit everyone. You can trust your judgement to help you find what works for you.

So - what helps? Put succinctly, this is most people's preferred option - *Getting the hell out of there!*

Of course. Most of our feelings of fear reduce rapidly once we are out of the confined space, although feelings of shakiness may take a while to subside. This is very good news, and a fact worth using when we feel trapped, to challenge the panicky thought/sense that the terrible feelings are never going to end. It's the kind of thing that mothers say to comfort children having injections - *"It's alright, it'll be over soon, you'll be fine"*. In other words, *"This too will pass"*.

This chapter provides many alternatives to simple avoidance, to help you handle claustrophobia. You'll find strategies focused on physical, mental/cognitive and emotional aspects of life, and finding support through relationships and creativity (arranged alphabetically opposite). You'll find further ideas in Chapter 10, *Finding Support through Therapy*.

Self-help strategies arranged alphabetically

Assessment of risk, and self-trust p. 119

Breaking the challenge down into steps p. 122

Breathing p. 109

Buddies p. 143

Calm packs p. 149

Creative expression p. 150

Curiosity p. 128

Diaries of success p. 123

Distraction p. 151

Exercise and fitness p. 112

Films and TV - using fantasy constructively p. 158

Freedom p. 163

Laughter and humour p. 130

Mindfulness p. 164

Nutrition p. 115

Physical contact p. 147

Planning p. 124

Positive experiences p. 131

Practising p. 134

Rebellion and being assertive p. 135

Relaxation p. 116

Resilience p. 165

Rewards, celebration and the contribution we make p. 167

Roles p. 170

Routine p. 117

Secure base p. 148

Self-soothing p. 136

Sleep p. 118

Stay a little longer p. 137

Support networks p. 148

Taking breaks p. 137

Thought replacement and thought stopping p. 127

Visualisation p. 171

Voice of calm p. 138

PHYSICAL STRATEGIES

BREATHING

"Slow breathing to try to calm the physical sensations. I try to keep my mind blank and not let the negative thoughts build up"

"Breathing properly and not allowing the feelings to escalate"

If we feel anxious, our breathing rate tends to increase and become ragged. Taking deep breaths at this point is not necessarily helpful, as we may run the risk of hyperventilating, and raising our panic levels. Deep breathing is also unhelpful if there is anything in the atmosphere that shouldn't be inhaled. It's easy to (mis)-interpret any problems with breathing as catastrophic, whereas they are mostly simply uncomfortable and can be resolved quite quickly.

It may be more helpful to concentrate on *steadying* and *slowing* our breathing, rather than controlling or trying to deepen it, focusing on the air passing out of and into our noses. Controlling sounds rather tight-lipped and rigid! - the last things we want to be if we want to return to a calm, grounded state of relaxed awareness. A focus on *lengthening* the amount of time we hold breaths and between breaths is probably more effective than focusing solely on the in-breath, which will return to a natural rhythm, once the diaphragm is relaxed.

Breathing into a paper bag is a classic standby for regulating breathing (*note* - not a plastic bag). The bag contains our out-breath, so the concentration of carbon dioxide in the air we inhale increases. This has a relaxing effect as it passes into our bloodstream. The warmth of our breath on our face is also soothing, as may be the knowledge that we are doing something practical to help ourselves.

Slow breathing is helpful if you want to relax before or during time in a confined space, if you are practising positive visualisation (*see* p. 171) or planning another experiment. Learning to 'body breathe' can also be helpful.

BODY BREATHING

Relax your shoulders, and place your hands on your lower belly. Your aim is to draw the air downwards, imagining that it is flowing into your lungs, through your diaphragm, into your stomach so much so that your belly rises, pushing your hands up and out. Your shoulders should not rise, but stay relaxed. If you find it hard at first, try pressing down with your hands on your belly, as you breathe out, almost as if you are expelling the air. Then, as the air comes in, see if you can allow the next breath to push your stomach up and out. Repeating a cycle of taking a long slow breath, holding it for a couple of moments, releasing it with a slight sound (fffffffff...) and then pausing for a moment before the next breath, can create a deep sense of relaxation.

Once you are happy with body breathing in this way, you can add in creative visualisation (p. 171) or positive affirmations. As with hypnosis, your body's state of warm relaxation will allow you access to deeper, more receptive layers of consciousness. Following this kind of breathing, you may want to 'visit' your entire body from toe to scalp, to release any tension you may find there (see *Relaxation* p. 116 and *Mindfulness* p. 164)

Thich Nhat Hanh and Rachel Neuman suggest following this cycle of breath and thought (in *Calming the Fearful Mind*, 2005, Parallax Press):

I	Breathing in	allow the thought	–	I am aware of my feelings
2	Breathing out	allow the thought	–	I calm and release the tension of my feelings
3	Breathing in	allow the thought	–	I know I am alive
4	Breathing out	allow the thought	–	I smile at life

A lovely aspect of this cycle is the almost irresistible urge to smile after the fourth line. Smiling triggers positive hormones, feelings and memories, and is worth doing for its own sake, whatever else is happening.

EXERCISE AND FITNESS

Becoming physically fit or fitter through increased activity and exercise has multiple benefits for those of us who experience claustrophobia. Exercise reduces the likelihood of heart disease and strokes, lowers blood pressure and muscular tension, and builds and maintains healthy muscles, bones and joints. It's a brilliant outlet for frustration and aggression, the kind of feelings you don't want to find yourself full of if the lift stops between floors. Our sense of ourselves as robust, optimistic, resilient individuals increases.

Exercise rids our systems of the unhealthy build-up of stress hormones, and stimulates the release of chemicals that are known to reduce depression and anxiety. It aids sleep and promotes relaxation, both in turn more likely to enable us to think more clearly. If an incident or accident does happen in a confined space or anywhere else, the likelihood of experiencing profound trauma (or PTSD) can be related to how anxious or depressed you were at the time. So anything we can do to reduce these feelings before we go into confined spaces, is helpful. Physical activity can be both fun and sociable, enriching our general sense of well-being and building our sense of attachment to other people and the world at large. *It may be advisable to get medical advice before taking up a new form of exercise, and to remember the importance of warming up before activity and cooling down afterwards.*

Any old exercise will help, but it's worth considering being active out-of-doors, whether through organised sport, gardening, cycling, walking, riding, geocaching, conservation work and so on. All these activities could be described as 'Green Exercise', a term coined by Dr. Jules Pretty of the University of Essex and colleagues (www.essex.ac.uk/bs/staff/pretty/green_ex.shtm).

Their research has shown that the benefits of exercise and the benefits of being in nature mutually enhance each other, leading to lower blood pressure and greater self-esteem than if exercise is taken solely indoors, say in a gym setting. In addition, if we exercise in the open air, we're giving ourselves all the pleasures of the kinds of places we prefer to the confined places we'd rather avoid. So we can build up our internal portfolio of sensory imagery to access if we get or feel trapped.

Physical strength and speed can bring confidence in themselves, in that we're more likely to be able to look after ourselves and other people if we had to. Another advantage of exercise out-of-doors is that we will be exposed to sunlight. People who experience Seasonal Affective Disorder are known to have an improvement in symptoms with exposure to light, especially certain frequencies available early in the day. There could be aspects of SAD symptomology within our claustrophobic response - so counter the possibility with bucketfuls of daylight.

Fitness alone does not guarantee we won't experience claustrophobia, or the effects of trauma. Sports people as well as classic couch potatoes have felt profound anxiety in confined spaces. Nonetheless, improving our health and well-being is likely to leave us stronger and more relaxed, and thus more able to take on the challenges that overcoming claustrophobia throws up.

Think about how athletes, tennis players and sports people of all disciplines prepare themselves for major competitions. They don't leave their feelings to chance. They spend time concentrating on 'psyching themselves up'. They think about past achievements, and the training they have put in to prepare themselves for the event. They relax into the moment, with warm-up movements which they have practised and worked into a reliable familiar routine. They focus; they get themselves into 'the zone', a self-induced almost hypnotic state that reduces their world to the task in hand. They look ahead, visualising themselves in minute detail, seeing themselves succeed at every step of the race or challenge to come.

And once they start to play, they let go of any mistakes. To dwell on a mistake or failure is to lose the moment, become snagged on a mental thorn of regret, and their concentration and full awareness of the task-in-hand are broken. To succeed, they have to let it go. The best sports people of all kinds visualise winning, and the intense physical, emotional and mental pleasure they will experience when they do. If they're part of a team, sportsmen and women encourage and motivate each other. They get positive feelings flowing between them, and they build each other up, as well as themselves. The epitome of energetic team-building must be the New Zealand All Blacks, doing the Haka, filling themselves with passion and unstoppable power through their movements, facial gestures and chanting.

We might not feel like doing a Haka before we contemplate going for an MRI scan or driving into an underground car-park or taking a flight, but we could. We could devise our own physical, facial, vocal routine and practice it. We could find fabulous, uplifting songs, and sing them out loud whilst moving in a powerful, rhythmical way. Even a long-strided walk will do, using both sides of your body and brain in balance, but it could be dancing, stamping, clapping, anything that involves our whole bodies, makes us breathe deeply and sends blood shooting round our bodies to oxygenate and invigorate even the most neglected corners. We could embolden ourselves to know that we can defeat the 'enemy', whether we see that as the small space we're trying to go into, or the voices of dread in our heads. And what we can achieve is a deep sense of pride, calm, confident, sustaining pride in ourselves and our bodies.

NUTRITION

When you're working on overcoming claustrophobia, think about the kinds of foods that can help you. Do what your mum said, have breakfast! Light, regular meals featuring protein and slow-release carbohydrates are more sustaining and brain-nourishing than quick-fix sugar-based foods and drinks. These produce a 'high' which might be temporarily encouraging, but can be followed by the depressive slump as sugar levels in the bloodstream fall again, the last thing you need just as you get back on the underground or if the lift suddenly stops between floors. So keep the chocolate as a reward for *after* your experiment. Equally, gearing yourself up with strong coffee or overuse of alcohol is likely to be counter-productive. Both are likely to lead to physical and emotional symptoms that can undermine you, creating agitation, over-reactiveness, and/or confusion. They are also more likely to make an anxious stomach more queasy and easily upset.

Above all, keep hydrated. Sometimes feeling thirsty is a late symptom of dehydration - irritability, problems with concentration, tension, even mild signs of anxiety can all be traced to insufficient water. Our minds feel clearer, our bodies feel more relaxed when we've drunk adequate water. It's your body where you've felt the effects of claustrophobia. Whatever you can do to maintain its stability and well-being will help.

RELAXATION

A very simple way of achieving muscular relaxation is to pick one specific group of muscles, say in the hand, and then either stretch them - and hold, hold for a couple of beats - and then relax them. Or tense them (in a fist) - and hold for a couple of beats - and then relax them. As the muscles relax, the build-up of blood held back by the tension washes through, like a river through a log-jam, and your hand will be more relaxed than before.

A systematic relaxation process would involve following this procedure all the way through your body - starting with your toes, then your instep - then your heel and ankle, then your whole foot, then your calf - and so on up the body, including your face and scalp. If you yawn whilst you're doing it, all to the good. It means both that you're relaxing and taking in more air. Closing your eyes whilst you take your mind through your body in this way facilitates even deeper relaxation. A second form of body relaxation is to stroke down your own upper arms, forearms and hands. Imagining the tension leaving your finger-tips as you stroke can be both de-stressing and soothing. Firm, slow, downward strokes work best. See if you can allow the stroking hand to relax as well.

Yoga, meditation, mindfulness practice, music, painting, time spent quietly outdoors listening to the sounds of nature and letting ourselves be simple, can all increase our access to wonderful states of relaxation. As can more active approaches: a great game of tennis or football, hill-walking, sailing, boisterous time with friends and family and animals - the list is endless, and each of us has our own preferred methods. The key is to find what works, build regular time for it into busy lives, and allow ourselves to fully experience the richness of relaxation, be fully present in the moment in our bodies. This way, we not only reduce the likelihood of being further traumatised by stressful experiences, but we also form deep, sensory images of the state of relaxation, which we can access in times of tension.

Finally, massage can be helpful, both in creating a deep feeling of relaxation, as well as in allowing ourselves to be cared for. Claustrophobia can bite deep, leaving body memories of vulnerablility, hurt and scare. Being touched kindly and with care can heal that hurt, reconnecting us to ourselves and the pleasures of our bodies.

ROUTINE

If your claustrophobia came about as the result of a recent trauma, then re-establishing your previous routine as quickly as possible has been shown to be effective in helping overcome the effects. Others of us are working on claustrophobia that started some time ago, or that we have had all our lives. Routine can help here by providing stability whilst we expose ourselves to the potential turbulence of facing difficult feelings.

In other words, you may give yourself a better chance of making real progress with your claustrophobia if you have a fairly normal stretch of weeks ahead of you, rather than holidays, Christmas, or if something else of major or stressful significance is happening, like a house or job move.

SLEEP

The restorative power of sleep is enormous. If you're experimenting with going back into confined spaces, try it when you're rested and well-slept. You may be making life harder for yourself if you start experimenting when you're already feeling a bit ragged after a series of late nights or very early mornings, just after the clocks go back or forward, if you've swapped time zones, if you have jet-lag or even if you've simply flown recently. Of course sometimes we'll be in confined spaces already feeling rough, for a variety of reasons, and gradually we can learn to cope with that. But don't shoot yourself in the foot by starting that way!

After an experiment, you may feel very tired. You've probably 'geared yourself up' for your next bold adventure, and it's completely normal to complete the cycle of action through rest. In fact, if you're feeling good about what you've achieved, your sense of tiredness may be surprisingly pleasant: a refreshing, all-body experience of sleepiness rather than the leaden tiredness that comes with anxiety and feeling low.

Conversely, you may feel quite agitated and not be able to sleep. Some people whose claustrophobia came about through trauma, or through displacement from other anxiety-provoking issues, may experience flashbacks or unexpected feelings or new thoughts. Going back to the places and spaces you've avoided can 'stir up' your psyche, a kind of *aftermath* effect, as Geoff Thompson describes it (see Resources).

If this happens, be gentle with yourself. Go to or imagine going to your *secure ba*se (p. 148), keep warm, talk to people who care about you. Contain the thoughts in a racing brain by writing them down as they come into your mind, to look at more calmly later, or paint them. Try simple *relaxation* (p. 116), *self-soothing* (p. 136) and *breathing* techniques (p. 109). Look after yourself. Remind yourself that you are safe, and that you can find the support you need.

If you become very sleepless whilst working on your claustrophobia, it's probably a sign that you are going too fast. Slow down. Spend more time building your support systems and enjoy replenishing your supply of happy memories through real experience. Trust your intuition to know when you're ready to try another experiment.

MENTAL/COGNITIVE STRATEGIES

ASSESSMENT OF RISK AND SELF-TRUST

To develop our skills of risk assessment, we need to be clear about what we fear is going to happen if we go into a confined space. As people who experience claustrophobia, our bottom-line fear is usually that the confined situation will be fatal, either because we will be powerless to defend ourselves from actual threat, or because we'll become so frightened we'll have a heart or asthma attack. Lesser anxieties include feeling we *'won't be able to stand'* the feelings of fear in a non-specific way.

Once we're clear what we're worried about, we can then decide how likely each of those outcomes are, and whether we feel we have enough internal and external resources to risk facing them.

I am grateful to the contributor who taught me his mnemonic **FFR** - Factorise, Familiarise, Rationalise. This process enrols us as information seekers, researchers, makes use of our power of observation. To *factorise* is to identify each aspect of the situation we feel apprehensive about. To *familiarise* is to find out about and understand each aspect, in sufficient detail to enable us to *rationalise* - set fact and logic about the situation alongside our fantasies, and arrive at a rational conclusion about the risks involved and what we want to do. So, for example, you want to go into a car-wash:

1   How likely is that the car-wash will malfunction in such a way as to pose an actual physical threat? How can I find out? (Use FFR)

2   How likely is that my heart will give out or my breathing become difficult if I get very stressed? (seek medical advice if you feel you may have an underlying health problem, *and see* p. 31)

3   What resources do I have and what support is available, to help me cope with whatever happens and with whatever I feel?

This information can help you work out how best to approach the situation, when you're ready. Of course all the rationalising in the world isn't going to be helpful if we find it difficult to remember our conclusions once we start feeling anxious. We can't simply present clinical logic to our frightened hearts, and expect instant resolution of our fears. Which is why it's important to go slowly, to take small risks first, to gradually build the bridge between thought and feeling through concrete experience in the real world. The more compassionately we view our apprehension, the more likely we are to be able to use our assessment wisely.

SELF-TRUST

I realised when I was researching my book on overcoming procrastination that the habit of putting things off fundamentally undermines our trust in ourselves, and is destructive to confidence and self-esteem. After all, if a friend or colleague constantly promised to do something with or for you, and then, time after time, postponed that action, you'd pretty soon lose confidence in their ability to follow through. In time the basis of your relationship would be eroded. In a very similar way, if we keep breaking our own promises to ourselves, then at a deep level, we lose our belief that we will do what we have said we'll do, and that our words and intentions can be trusted.

If a friend had continually let you down, no amount of persuasion would instantly re-build your belief in their reliability. Again, it is the same with ourselves. To restore trust, and indeed to build trust we have never had, we have to go micro-step by micro-step, following through each intention reliably with concrete, tangible action in the real world. We need to set ourselves micro-tasks **not only** so that we don't frighten ourselves with too much too soon, **but also** so that we can build or re-build trust between the thinking and feeling parts of selves.

Trust, in the first instance, that the thinking part really can assess risks properly, can distinguish between fact and hypothesis. And that means acknowledging genuine risk as much as it means acknowledging our tendency to see inevitable catastrophe where the likelihood is very slim. For example, there is no point telling ourselves that travelling by centrally-locked car is one hundred percent completely safe, when it isn't, anymore than frightening ourselves by believing that the car will inevitably be involved in an accident - which it won't be. We should no more promise ourselves that the plane won't crash, that the car-wash won't ever malfunction, that the person with the bomb won't get on our train, than we should persuade ourselves that all these things *will* definitely happen. The key thing is not to false-promise yourself. The scared self needs to have constant evidence that the reassuring, guiding self is realistic and trustworthy.

The likelihood is that these horrible things won't happen. The probability is we will be entirely safe, fine and trauma-free, sometimes uncomfortable, sometimes a bit more scared than we'd like to be, if something happens. But to develop trust in ourselves, we need to recognise the grain of truth, acknowledge it, work out whether there are any other pre-disposing factors in either direction and make a judgement. These are skills we can build in everyday life, not only in confined places we'd rather avoid.

To re-build our trust in ourselves can be a slow process, requiring much patience, compassion, and love. We need to be gentle. And that is where we need to pay attention not only to what we say to ourselves, but also, how we say it (*see* Voice of reason, *below*)

BREAKING THE CHALLENGE DOWN INTO STEPS

Any of the challenges we set ourselves in overcoming claustrophobia can be broken down into stages - there are examples throughout this book. Sometimes these may require a little imagination, and some lateral thought. Sometimes you may need to strengthen your resilience in other areas of your life (developing social connections and support, restoring health, confidence in your ability to problem-solve and so on - *and see* p. 165) before taking one step into a confined space. This isn't avoidance. It's about care in preparation, building resources, and not putting yourself in a position to become further traumatised.

Only you can really decide what the next step will be, what would make the next incremental shift in the right direction. You'll know if the step is too large, by your own reaction to it. It's helpful to recognise that sometimes even being willing to contemplate or think about taking the next step is progress. Previously you may not have been able to contemplate an invitation to go to the theatre with a crowd of friends: now at least you're willing to discuss it. That's a step. Don't discount it. Allow yourself to register the change.

Some people find it helpful to use the acronym SMART as an aide memoire - breaking tasks down into challenges that are *Small, Measurable, Achievable, Realistic,* and completed within a particular *Time-frame.* So if one of your aims is to be able to use buses with electronically operated doors, for example, you might decide to take one bus, for one stop, during the next hour. Tick! Another step forward. You may have to do this many more times before you feel relaxed about it, but you've broken the ice, you're out of virgin territory.

Other people find deliberately planning a fixed time to take precisely the next step only serves to increase their anxiety, and would rather surprise themselves by taking a step when the moment is right. Either route will add to the memory bank of tangible, real-world experiences that your brain can use to modify its previous impression that such a step was too terrifying, or impossible.

DIARIES OF SUCCESS

When facing the next challenge, it's sometimes easy to forget the progress we've already made. Facing the next step up in the hierarchy of your anxieties can feel dishearteningly like being back at the beginning again.

In a way it is, in that it is the beginning of a new project; one beginning reminds us of all others, with the outcome just as uncertain. This is the same for many projects, not only overcoming fears - notice how many writers feel the same terror each time they face a blank page or empty screen! And, at the same time, it isn't - you've been through a beginning before, you're not a total beginner at going through beginnings.

A great way to remind yourself of this is to keep a 'diary of success'. Creating a log of all your different experiments provides you with concrete, incontrovertible evidence of the effort you've already put in, the courage you've already developed, the success you've already achieved. Reflecting on these past successes, no matter how small, can be enormously encouraging, reinforcing your image of yourself as someone with tenacity and resourcefulness, the qualities of resilience (*see below*).

In addition, it can help to remember that we've all been resourceful and dealt with difficulties, in situations other than confined spaces. Think back to any incident, and take note of what you did that helped yourself or others: include it in the diary. You can record your calmness and composure, your quick-wittedness, your strength, your imagination. Re-visiting and savouring those memories can help to maximise the possibility of further success in future.

PLANNING

" If I can do something independently to escape the situation
then I will plan my strategy in my head before acting. If

*I cannot escape the situation I go into my head and relax
myself and do not let it overpower me"*

As you prepare for an experiment towards your goal, a little planning
goes a long way.

MENTAL PREPARATION - WHAT THOUGHTS WILL HELP ME MOST?

Internal vista - past experiences of success: motivation for
overcoming claustrophobia; things you're looking forward to; how
you will feel when you successfully complete your experiment;
positive visualisations; how well you're doing; that this too will
pass.

External - plan to become mindful of the environment you're in,
how it was designed, how you would improve it: other people in
that environment, what they might be like, what they are wearing;
who they remind you of; what you imagine they'd like as a present;
how you would help that person if they needed you; how they might
be able to help you

PHYSICAL PREPARATION - HOW WILL I GROUND AND STEADY MYSELF?

Prepare yourself physically by planning what you could do to
restore calm and equilibrium. This could include focusing on
your breath gently going out and coming in through your nose:
pressing with your feet against the floor, one after the other, or
your hands against each other; tensing and relaxing different
groups of muscles in either a rhythmical adrenaline using-up way,
or in a relaxing way (*see Breathing & Relaxation in this section
for further ideas*).

EMOTIONAL PREPARATION - WHAT POSITIVE FEELINGS CAN I CREATE FOR MYSELF?

Plan to visualise your safe place and the smiling, loving faces of your support network (*see* p. 148). Give yourself permission to make contact with other people if you need to, what you might say, how you might say it. Here's how one contributor thinks through how she'll do this:

"If I need help, I will wait until I am calm enough to ask calmly, so it is a friendly request and not a panicked one."

ESCAPE PLANNING

Unless you are of the school of thought that says you must stay with your fear to the point at which it extinguishes, you may also wish to build in escape routes. This might mean - *I'll try going three floors in the lift, but I give myself permission to leave after two floors -I'll try going into the car-wash, but if I really can't, I'll spend time studying the process and learning more about it* - and so on. You'll know if you're over-using escape routes, if they are just becoming an avoidance. You'll also know if having one is helping you make progress. Trust your intution to know the difference.

PLANNING FOR GETTING STUCK

Thinking through what you'd do if you became trapped can be anxiety-provoking in itself. On the other hand, if we think through the range of alternatives we'd have, picture ourselves carrying them out effectively, they are more likely to come to mind if we need them. The more we have confidence that we can physically and mentally maintain our well-being if we do get stuck, the less we will fear becoming so. We may never quite reach Liz Hayward's idea that being trapped in a lift would be a welcome break! (p. 180) - but if you think through alternative strategies, you're giving yourself powerful messages that you are a capable and strong person, with a huge range of skills and interests, who has the resources to cope. You're not promising yourself you won't feel anxious - you might, anyone might - but your focus will be on being resourceful.

THOUGHT REPLACEMENT AND THOUGHT STOPPING

When our minds are filled and bubbling with anxiety-driven thoughts, it can be difficult for the voice of calm to get a look-in. Any practice we can do *outside* confined situations to shift our focus of attention will give us a greater sense of confidence in our ability to do so when times get tough. For some, this might mean the practice of mindfulness (p. 164). For others, this might mean thought replacement or thought stopping.

We all know how hard it is to tell yourself to stop worrying. Trying to suppress worries can even make them grow in significance or frequency. So we have some options. We can distract ourselves, re-direct our attention somewhere genuinely more interesting. We can ask ourselves whether the thought we are having is helping us to feel calm and settled, or if there is a more constructive thought that would work better.

We can challenge our assumptions, our generalisations, our black-and-white thinking, our internal critical saboteur, our drive towards being perfect. We can teach ourselves to think in terms of *preferences* (*I'd prefer not to feel anxious, but I'll survive*) rather than impossible-to-fulfil *imperatives* (*I must not feel anxious* *). We can actively look to see if there is any concrete irrefutable

* From *Three Minute Therapy* by Dr. Michael Edelstein (Glenbridge 1997)

evidence that things are going badly, rather than assume that we know that there will be. We can counter-balance negative thoughts with evidence of positive facts and possibilities. We can even 'ping' an elastic band on our wrists to remind ourselves to 'snap' out of our immersion in worry and fretting (although in a way this is a kind of punishment - personally I'm not pro treating anxiety with pain, but some people find it helpful as a kind of negative reinforcement). (*For more on working with thoughts, see* p. 204)

EMOTIONAL STRATEGIES

CURIOSITY

Curiosity is a function of allowing ourselves to notice what is around us, and to follow or focus on what triggers our interest. We're more likely to be curious when we feel safe, like a child who wants to get up and explore the park once she's been reassured that mum or dad is nearby. Paradoxically, we can help ourselves feel more secure by focusing on what stimulates our curiosity.

Curiosity is an open-ended, questioning stance, characterised by open-ended, experimental thinking or attitudes:

"I wonder what/what else/how/why/where/who/when/if......????"

rather than by judging or jumping to instant conclusions. It attunes us to and increases our knowledge of our environment. It can animate us with new interest. It enables us to compare and contrast, to notice what we are drawn to, what doesn't hold our attention.

Engaged curiosity indicates the arousal of the 'seeking system' in our brains. Of course if we're being hyper-vigilant, as many of us are when we feel anxious, we're already scanning our environment pretty rapidly, for clues that things are about to go terribly wrong, almost looking for validation of our fear, something to pin it on. Allowing ourselves to be *curious* about what we notice, rather than coming to instant and possibly erroneous conclusions, can strengthen our powers of cool reflection and discrimination. It makes use of our eyes, ears, senses, but from a relaxed stance, rather than a frantic one. Curiosity can transform the energy of anxiety into the energy of pleasure, and an eagerness to engage with the world. Curiosity can give us ideas for new goals and promote our enthusiasm for carrying them forward.

So Idris Williams, for example, the Training Officer of the British Caving Association takes people who are apprehensive about caves, but wanting to challenge their fear, on simple trips and interests them in the underground environment. He attempts to make them *"so involved that the claustrophobia is forgotten. A programme of increasingly more confined trips could follow to build up tolerance/experience"*. Here the energy stimulated by curiosity is used up in learning and acquiring new knowledge, making the trip more satisfying than frightening, and potentially leading to further exploration.

Of course curiosity has its limitations - we wouldn't have come far as a species if we had dwelt too long on wondering about the density of a woolly mammoth's coat! (or some historically more accurate species-threatening phenomenon). But it's another great tool for improving our ability to discriminate between our imagination and reality.

And we can hold the same attitude about ourselves and our reactions as well - as in,

I wonder how I will feel if I go in this cable car? ...
rather than -
> *I definitely* will *feel scared*
> (which could become a self-fulfilling prophecy)
> - *and that would be awful* (which it might not be)

or indeed,
> *I definitely* won't *feel scared*
> (which could also turn out to be untrue)

Curiosity and wondering keeps us alive and open to possibility, freshness, surprise, and learning, the antitheses of the stuck and frustrated feelings of claustrophobia.

LAUGHTER AND HUMOUR

In 2005, many bloggers referred to the humour passengers used in trying to maintain morale in the horrendous aftermath of the bombing on the London Underground, reminiscent perhaps of the famous Blitz spirit, fondly remembered by many from the Second World War. Humour at such times may have a dark edge to it, but it serves the same purpose. Brian Keenan, imprisoned for years in small cells, conveys in *An Evil Cradling* (Vintage, 1993) the huge joy and release he found in shared and private laughter, from dry irony, the relish of sharp wit, to hilarity, extraordinary under the circumstances.

Laughter lowers stress, boosting our immune systems, relaxing our muscles and releasing feel-good hormones; these positive effects can last quite a while after a good belly laugh. When we take life too seriously, try to find too much meaning in what's going on, try to stay in control, we can lose spontaneity and lock ourselves up in the kind of isolated, alienated world we fear we'll get stuck in inside confined spaces. Humour restores our perspective, reminding us that we are all fallible and probably gullible, and connects us to other people, reminding us we are not alone. Laughter makes us breathe more deeply and relax: we feel more confident, stronger, more compassionate, more able to take on the world. Humour converts adrenaline into feelings of excitement, which can be as contagious as anxiety*. Sometimes it's not even necessary to know why someone else is laughing to be able to join them, in shared delight. Memories of the joy of shared laughter make us smile and can brighten the present moment, however grim.

In short, humour and laughter are good for us - they are anti-claustrophobic. So find something to laugh about every day.

POSITIVE EXPERIENCES

We need a lot of these! Real world excitement, real world fun, putting the knowledge of pleasure deep into our bodies and into our memory archives, ready for access. William Bloom, in his marvellous book *Feeling Safe* (Piatkus, 2002) reminds us that to have access to memories of pleasure means that you need to have pleasurable experiences, and then remember them. This sounds obvious, but it can be all too easy not to notice the many wonderful things that happen in busy or demanding lives. So it means taking note when something good, lovely, marvellous, kind, hilarious, brilliant, or even just a bit nicer than normal is happening to you, in the real world, not in your imagination.

Stop in your tracks. Register that you are enjoying the moment; savour it. Notice what is happening with all your

*see Laughter therapy, in Resources

senses. What can you see, hear, smell, taste, touch? Who
is with you? What time of day is it? Where is the sun in
the sky? Where is the moon? What is the quality of light?
How warm or cold are you? Log this moment, in all its
richness and beauty.

My father has a great phrase for reminding his family to do this.
When we were on holiday as children, driving through beautiful
Devon countryside, standing on Cornish cliff-tops watching the sun
go down into a seemingly endless golden Atlantic, or even, once,
taking the 'second-longest unsupported cable car in Europe' (a
description also logged in the family phrase book) with stunning
views over alpine mountains, my father would command us all to
"Drink it all in!". And we did.

I can't remember the precise views we saw, but I remember
the sense, of wide open landscapes, of sky, sea, beaches, hillsides,
trees, salty sea air, the sun warming our faces … such pleasures
nurture me now, when I remember to remember, wherever I am.

One of the key body chemicals responsible for our good
feelings is dopamine. When dopamine is flowing well in our brains
we feel energised, alert, able to experience pleasure and happiness,
motivated, curious, open to learning, and excited; we are ALIVE
and we feel it. The world seems an inviting, fascinating place; we
feel its welcome and we want to jump right in.

Without dopamine, we're likely to feel lethargic, indecisive,
lacking in curiosity, and miserable to the point of depression
(Sunderland 2006). The world seems to shrink, to become dark and
empty. People who experience claustrophobia already experience
aspects of the world as 'shrunken' and threatening. We don't want
to compound the problem by reinforcing the gloom. So how to
generate a healthy flow of 'feel good' hormones?

A very simple way is to 'count our blessings'. We all have blessings, regardless of our circumstances. Seeking them out in our mind's eye may activate pleasure centres in our brains, triggering the release of feel-good hormones.

A blessing can be as simple (and incredible) as being able to see. Being able to notice colour. Being able to hear. Being able to move. Being able to remember a friend's face, or to see it, or to stroke it. Remembering times of happiness, great conversations, beautiful views, moments of tenderness, of warmth, pride, joy, success, fun, of ecstasy even, and being grateful for them. Re-visiting everything that we love and that makes us happy, and appreciating all of it.

You could make a list of all these things to take into the next confined space you want to enter. You could put the list in the sunniest place in your house, and ask your friends and family to add their favourite words to it. And then, when you're in the confined space, picture that place and the sunshine and the wonderful people you know. Then, look around the environment you are actually in and see what else you could add to the list.

In *An Evil Cradling* (Vintage 1993) Brian Keenan writes very movingly about the one occasion when he was given fruit. He didn't eat it - the lustrous beauty of the fruit in the unbelievable bleakness of his prison environment was so awe-inspiring, such a reminder of everything that is good in life, and so unspoilt, that he wanted to keep and cherish it as long as possible.

It doesn't matter how small the blessings are, the key thing is to start noticing them, in your mind, on paper, in conversation, in song, however you like. The more you notice, the more you'll find.

The more you notice, the more your positive feelings will flow.

The great joy of this strategy is that it is free, completely portable, can be done in a second, and requires no additional props whatsoever. It can be done anywhere, at any time, in a split second or for hours. Not only will it give you access to wonderful feelings from the past, but it will also prepare your body and brain for greater enjoyment of the present moment. It will help you to experience the world as inviting, rather than threatening. It sounds almost too good to be legal!

PRACTISING DEALING WITH FEAR

Anytime we take a risk, in any area of our lives, we may experience the adrenaline rush of fear or anxiety. *Fortunately for us, fear is fear is fear.* By which I mean, the fear we feel in claustrophobia is no different to any other kind of fear. This is excellent news. It means that if we practise dealing with fear, whether through building tolerance or by self-soothing, in situations unrelated to confined spaces, we can develop resilience against claustrophobia as well.

In the face of fear we want to fly, to fight the threat, or we freeze. If we can develop the ability to resist all three impulses, 'contain' the feelings and continue to be able to think about our experience, we have the chance of choosing the most appropriate way to respond to what is happening. These skills are transferable.

Eventually, we'll want to try going back to the confined or crowded places we've been avoiding, but as practice, doing anything else we're apprehensive about is going to help. Experiencing claustrophobia is not a separate thing in itself. It's something we can approach laterally, cunningly, even mischievously, and get on top of. We don't have to suffer as much as we might think. *The world is our practice oyster.*

REBELLION AND BEING ASSERTIVE

If a building or service won't accommodate your difficulty in dealing with a confined space, it's worth remembering these two minor acts of resistance:

"I asked at the kiosk if I could go through the exit as I was claustrophobic (to avoid a long crowded corridor*). This was refused. As I thought this was unreasonable I just went through the exit when she was serving another customer"*

"At the airport they were making people take a really crowded lift, even though there was a perfectly good escalator that we normally use. I was already anxious about flying, I didn't need to add to it, so I said to the man, "What if you're claustrophobic?" - and he looked sheepish and let me through, so it can't have been essential to go by lift. I felt really good that I'd been assertive"

Sometimes you know there are no alternatives. If you want to go scuba-diving, you'll have to wear a mask, and yes, dammit, the Channel Tunnel will continue to go under the Channel. But protesting against systems that put humans into or through unnecessarily uncomfortable spaces can create positive change, and not just for people who experience claustrophobia. We open a world of possibility when we're willing to name our feelings, recognise when they have validity and look for fresh options, for ourselves as well as others.

We're also giving the scared part of ourselves a clear message that we are prepared to act on our own behalf, that we won't put ourselves into difficult situations for no good reason. Like a child whose parent stands up to another adult who has been abusive, the scared part will lap this message up, know that its concerns are respected, and feel ever more confident and safe.

SELF-SOOTHING

We know how to soothe. We know how to calm. Soothing another person can also be a way of soothing ourselves. We stroke their arms, their hair, long, relaxing, downward strokes. When we're trying to calm a child or an adult, we know to say *"There, there"*: we don't simply say *"there"*. We have an innate understanding of the soothing qualities of repetition. We use falling inflexion between the repetitions. We are literally talking the person down, from the height of their agitation to a lower, calmer pitch, using our voices. We instinctively soften our tone and speak quietly.

We know how to soothe another person. We can use the same loving tones, the same stroking with hand or voice, to soothe ourselves (*there's more about the power of the human voice - and our own internal voice - on p. 138*). Writing beautifully, in *Feeling Safe*, (Piatkus 2002) William Bloom describes this process as the practice of an 'internal kindness', in which we accept, cradle and fully acknowledge our distress: '*the mind becoming the caring parent to the body*'. Even thinking about this process can be relaxing.

STAY A LITTLE LONGER ...

"A hero is one who knows how to hang on one minute longer"
Norwegian Proverb

When we're learning how to tolerate fear, we need to be gentle with ourselves. Anxiety is a savage emotion: in undoing its effects, there is no need to adopt its tactics. If you managed to stay in the dentist's chair one minute longer, been willing to keep that helmet or breathing apparatus on for a moment more, gone down that windowless corridor one step further, managed one more moment of self-soothing, that's a real, tangible, *no-one-can-take-it-away-from-you* achievement.

Don't undermine it by telling yourself that *you're progressing too slowly, should be 'better' by now, ought to be braver.* You're doing fine.

TAKING BREAKS

In some therapies, you may be asked to regularly assess the progress and improvement you are making.

> *"I had a real problem trying to improve my score each session. Some weeks I was just too tired or too busy to do the homework. I don't think it was real avoidance, it was just life."*

If you're working through a hierarchy of situations you find difficult, it's easy to feel you have to keep pressing on all the time to more and bigger challenges. It can become a tyranny. It really is OK not to push yourself all the time. Once you start on the track of dealing with your avoidance, you're not condemned to walk on it constantly. Sometimes you might just want to give yourself a break: get someone else to take the car to the car-wash, take the stairs rather than make yourself take the lift (good for your heart and figure anyway), or ask someone else to go down to the cellar for the suitcases.

Because sometimes we may be just too stressed, emotionally upset for other reasons, or hormonally out-of-kilter. We may have been burning the candle a bit or not eaten enough regular brain-stabilising food. Sometimes we simply just get fed up with having to keep making the effort to overcome our difficulties. These are all times when we need to be kindest to ourselves, to do whatever is necessary at that time to bring ourselves back to a state of balance. Trust yourself to know the difference between a return to out-and-out avoidance, and a natural need to give yourself a break in the process. Driving yourself through sheer will-power is unlikely to achieve healing.

VOICE OF CALM, VOICE OF REASON

Once when I was in a plane taking off into a particularly turbulent November sky I heard a man in the seat behind talking his daughter through all the different stages of the lift-off.

> *"Now the pilot is letting the engine take us forward, that's the big noise: let's count together ... now we're going up, the wheels are being tucked inside, that's that sound - now look at the wings, see how the pilot is starting to turn..."*

Focusing on this man's voice helped me stay marginally in control of my terror. As the plane dipped, bucked and slid sideways, it was reassuring that at least someone who knew something about flying thought that nothing untoward was happening (since in my equally turbulent mind, we were seconds from disaster). Or at least if this man was worried, then he retained enough composure to be able to keep it out of his voice as he described what was happening to his daughter.

I felt very fortunate to have been sitting so near him, and after the flight, queuing at passport control, I went over to thank him. To my surprise, other people in the queue nodded and agreed - they had heard him too, and his words had helped. He had inadvertently created a small island of calm around Seat 16D, in a sea of distinct anxiety.

That man's little daughter will grow up with her father's voice as part of her thinking self. She'll internalise it, and probably forget later that it was her father who helped her feel safe and confident when she flies. If we haven't had similar voices, or if the trust we had in them became strained or broken, we can still learn to internalise helpful voices all our lives. We can constantly update our thinking selves, enabling them to provide a more reliable and quietly confident source of support for our feeling self. My memory of this man has lasted me far longer than that flight.

Such is the power of the human voice. But what about the content? On another occasion, a friend sat next to me through turbulence, bouncing in her seat, laughing maniacally and saying *"We're all going to die!"* - which helped considerably less (I *believe* she was trying to make me laugh). So it's not just any voice saying anything. It has to be a certain kind of tone, and convey calm information with authority. We can learn to develop this tone in how we speak to ourselves, and find the words that will help.

Developing an internal voice

> *"We stopped panicking by talking to each other and the driver started talking to us - we calmed each other down and listened to the driver - we passed the message* (that passengers would be led to safety through the tunnel once the electric tracks had been turned off) *down* (the train)"
> Rachel North, from *Out of the Tunnel* (Friday Books, 2007), on how passengers on the King's Cross underground train calmed each other on 7th July 2005.

As babies, we need the warmth and touch of our parents' arms and hands to soothe our distress when we are frightened or upset. Generally, one parent - usually our mother - becomes the person whose presence and touch we seek, whose warm arms and calm voice have the greatest reassuring effect. By holding us and saying soothing things, she gives us a feeling of security, even when we are far too young to know why we are anxious or what her words mean.

When she is there, we no longer feel like a tiny molecule lost in a vast ocean. When she holds us, her arms and voice 'contain' our anxiety. In other words, we find that although our little bodies are flooded with terror which feels never-ending, there is something - someone - outside us, who is not rocked by the waves of our panic, nor knocked over by the winds of our anxiety. She is bigger than whatever causes our fear. No wonder we need her. No wonder we relax when she is there.

Over time, with repeated experience of our anxiety being calmed by this caring person, we develop the capacity to be soothed by her voice alone (although most of us never lose the capacity to appreciate the reassurance of a kind, calm hand). The sound of her voice becomes a substitute for her reassuring presence, as holding and containing of us as her arms were. So instead of needing a cuddle to help us calm down after waking from a nightmare, our mother's voice calling from her bedroom may be enough to help us go back to sleep.

And also over time, we find other people who can give us that same sense of safety and confidence, maybe even more effectively than our mother could. We become able to feel secure away from home, and to be able to move out into the world. We learn to identify the kind of people whose presence helps us feel secure. And we learn to talk to ourselves, to use our own voice to soothe our anxieties.

So it follows that we need to strengthen this ability, if we are to believe ourselves in the middle of a claustrophobic panic (especially if no other voice is talking to us at that moment). It's probably unrealistic to imagine that we can reliably 'conjure up' a sufficiently calm, reassuring, encouraging, kind voice at times of tension, if we can't speak to ourselves in these kinds of tones at other times, when we're not feeling frightened. It may be something we need to practise.

Of course people speak to themselves in different ways, at different times. Listening to our self-talk can give us a clue to the kind of internal world we live in, which naturally has an effect on how we view the outside world, and how we live in it.

What kind of voice do you use when you speak to yourself?

Kind? Practical? Curious? Demanding, judgemental, accusing?

Supportive, warm, excited? Relaxed or anxiety-creating? Grim or funny? Cynical or hopeful?

Chaotic or orderly? Depressing or inspiring?

Distant or intimate? Scornful and harsh, or loving and encouraging?

For a week, listen into your internal voice and notice how it changes as you encounter different experiences. Notice whether your internal voice changes if you feel yourself becoming anxious.

Write down some of the things you notice you say to yourself when you are feeling anxious, or after the experience of being anxious. Write down some of the words you use, and try to describe the tone (see above for some suggestions).

Look at this list.

Does what you say help you in that situation? Is the tone helpful? If you were speaking to someone whom you wanted to encourage and support, would you use the same words and tone? Would you say the same things to your best friend?

If you notice that you speak aggressively or frantically to yourself, what alternative words could you use? What kinder language or tone could you use?

Next to the words you have written in the list above, write down some alternative words and describe the kind of tone you'd like to hear.

The key word here is CHERISH.

If you **cherished** yourself, how would you speak to yourself?

How we talk to ourselves at times when we are *not* experiencing claustrophobia is just as important as how we speak internally when we are feeling trapped. If you regularly drive yourself with a judgmental, critical voice, or tell yourself frightening things about the world, then you are less likely to be able to access the kind of voice you need when times get tough. Your feeling self is less likely to trust a critical thinking self to make accurate judgements about what is safe, than a thinking self that is generally supportive and encouraging.

So whatever self-help strategy we decide to try, whichever therapy you go for, strengthening your ability to trust yourself, and to talk to yourself in loving ways will stand you in good stead. You will be more likely to be able to deal with uncomfortable feelings, more able to return to a position of relaxed awareness, more able to make good decisions on the basis of cool judgement. More able to listen to that little steadying inner voice. And less claustrophobic.

RELATIONSHIPS

BUDDIES

The experience of claustrophobia can be very lonely, so finding a buddy to support your return to confined spaces can be enormously helpful. There are two kinds:

BUDDY TYPE 1 Someone who also experiences claustrophobia, and who also wants to overcome it
This person is likely to understand you! Knowing claustrophobic panic for themselves from the inside, this kind of buddy has a good idea what you've been going through, and won't belittle you or your anxiety. Being able to share fears and experiences with someone who can sincerely empathise can help to reduce the shame we may sometimes feel about 'being claustrophobic'. Members

of the National Phobics Society (*see Resources*), for example, draw strength from knowing that they are not alone in anxiety, that others also have these fears, and, indeed, may have found ways to overcome them.

This kind of buddy knows the depth of courage it takes to begin to face your fears. They can cheer you on, be interested in the tiny steps of progress you make, and celebrate your success. And you can support them, too. Your own difficult experiences have enabled you to develop empathy. You can translate previous fear into a positive contribution towards someone else's progress.

Ideally, you will be able to support each other in trying out things that are difficult for you both. A friend came with me to a Mind, Body and Spirit event where I was running a workshop, and we 'dared' each other to take the lift. It was very small, but had mirrors, so we made faces at ourselves, held hands and sang loudly all the way down. Fortunately we had the lift to ourselves!

This memory has helped me in other lifts, at other times. We have an ongoing conversation about who we would want in a lift with us if we ever got stuck (regrettably for her, Daniel Craig as James Bond is in mine). The *"Who would you like in your lift?"* game (*see* p. 178) helps us to associates lifts with pleasurable alternative scenarios as well as making us laugh, which is good in itself. Not all tactics for overcoming claustrophobia have to be serious and hard-going.

On the other hand... Talking about your experiences of claustrophobia with someone else who also feels claustrophobic can create anxieties where they didn't exist before. I became acutely aware of this when I started telling people about my experiences in the Channel Tunnel, and realised that I had to be sensitive about who I told what had happened. If conversations between you heighten your anxiety, without motivating you both to do anything about making progress to overcome your fear of confined spaces, then stop. You could run the risk of re-traumatising yourselves, or giving yourself ideas of new things to worry about.

A second disadvantage of a buddy who experiences claustrophobia themselves is that one of you may end up supporting the other rather than building your own tolerance of anxiety. Of course looking after someone else can be a great distraction! - but it could add to the anxiety of the situation for you unnecessarily, and put you off. A third consideration is that you may inadvertently hold each other back, by being over-protective of one another, or cautious. You may find that you collude with each other's avoidance, 'normalising' the phobic element of your anxiety - *"If you feel like this as well, it must be true!"*.

If you want to try something even a bit bold to challenge your phobic anxiety, the best kind of buddy will encourage you, not warn you of all the possible drawbacks. Unspoken envy can creep in here - we're all capable of being competitive, even about progress in overcoming fears! So make a pact that the proof of buddying each other successfully is in the progress you both make, rather than building a shelter together against perceived threats.

BUDDY TYPE 2 **Someone who doesn't experience claustrophobia, but who is willing to help you overcome it**
The best thing about this kind of buddy is that they won't get scared by the same things you do! - so you won't need to look after them (at least not until there's a spider in the bath …). They may well be able to help you hold onto your thinking, soothe you, help you to relax or distract you. All of these things may give you experiences you have been avoiding, paving the way back to independence. The best of buddies who don't experience claustrophobia are

those who recognise that not all your anxiety is irrational; who can respond to your fears with empathy and good humour: who have solid confidence in you, respect for your ability to make the changes you want, and a firm belief that change is possible. And preferably, have strong hands that can withstand being gripped.

On the other hand ... It's important to only allow yourself to be helped when you are ready, at your pace, to your agenda, not anyone else's. A buddy who doesn't experience claustrophobia may not fully understand that whilst your anxiety seems unrealistic to them, it feels very real to you. With the best intentions in the world, they may try to push you. Conversely, they may not realise when you feel more able to cope alone! - and be over-protective or rescuing, just as you were beginning to relax and feel safe in yourself. It's not possible for even the best of buddies to "get it right" all the time, which gives us plenty of practice in being clear about our needs and learning to tolerate being (slightly) out of control.

GOING SOLO

A final thought about both kinds of buddies is that if you build your sense of safety by, for example, always having this person with you when you go by lift or plane, or always thinking you could phone this buddy if you needed to, then you may panic and regress if that person is not available to you. This doesn't mean you haven't made inroads on your fear. If you were too afraid to travel by train or go to the theatre at all, and you've now done that with this person alongside you, don't discount the huge progress you've already made. But see having a buddy as a step on the way to overcoming claustrophobia, not a final solution.

Think of small steps you could take away from your reliance on this one person. This could include travelling in separate compartments of the same train; taking successive trains and agreeing to both get out and meet at the next station; travelling with someone else; travelling alone with a picture of that person or a note from them in your pocket; travelling alone without a picture or a note and imagining that the person is with you, in your mind's eye: travelling alone and allowing yourself to notice that you are alone.

The more experience you have had with your buddy, and the warmer the relationship, the more you can draw on the memories of your experiences together when you are alone, if you wish to. You may choose to expose yourself to the full force of your anxiety, knowing that you can survive it, or you may choose to soothe yourself with these happy memories. You have the choice; you can work out what works for you.

PHYSICAL CONTACT

Physical contact with someone else can be incredibly helpful at many stages in our journey back into confined spaces. Human beings are 'hard-wired' to seek physical proximity and comfort when we're anxious, and although that instinct may be socialised out of us to a large extent, fear can bring it back in an instant. When all else fails, as Rachel North says in her book, *Out of the Tunnel*, (Friday Books 2007), *"We can all hold hands in the dark"*. And we do - when we're scared, if we anticipate danger, if a disaster happens, and afterwards, or when bad news comes, we hold hands, we hold each other. And it helps.

My husband has lost count of the times when my tense fingers have left a deep imprint in his arm on planes, in lifts, in tunnels! And as I gradually became able to manage my own feelings better, my task was to see if I could hold his arm more lightly - hold his arm for less time - hold my own arm - if I can relax without *holding anything*. Each tiny step another success.

SECURE BASE

*"When I began therapy, I gradually overcame (my anxiety)
     by going into shops with my husband, leaving him at a
     given spot and gradually expanding my 'safety zone'
     away from him."*

Look back at the exercise on p. 16, and spend some time re-charging
your batteries in your 'secure base'. You can make great use of
this place as you overcome claustrophobia, in reality or through
visualisation. At the planning stage, you can use it as a place to start
from or to return to. When you're in the confined place you've been
avoiding, you can imagine your secure base or see yourself running
back to it (*see* Visualisation, *below*), and taste the wonderful sense
of relaxation you find there.

SUPPORT NETWORKS

As mentioned below in *Resilience,* humans tend to do better in the
world when they have a sense of belonging. Most of us probably fall
somewhere on the continuum between the two polarities described
on p. 58: we are neither completely secure nor completely insecure.
Early patterns of insecurity can be modified by later positive
experiences in relationships. But equally, trauma, experienced in a
claustrophobic situation or not, can temporarily disrupt or fragment
our core sense of security.

Whatever we can do to move in the direction of strengthening
our bonds with other people will be of assistance: talking, sharing

our experience, allowing ourselves to be known and cared for, problem solving together. And it needn't all be about difficulties - it's essential to build or re-build our relationships through sharing fun, laughter and pleasure. What better way to defy claustrophobic fears of separation and isolation?

But this can be very hard, and take time, especially if our background was already insecure. We will almost undoubtedly need support; our hurt needs to be repaired in relationship with other people. There is no shame to be had in asking for support, personal or professional; on the contrary, it's an ability the most resilient people have.

Good friends give you a hug and hold your hand. Good friends sing to you in the lift and make jokes in the underground. They give you their photograph or write messages of support on lovely cards, which you can take with you on your next experiment (you may have to ask for this). When we have a good support network, we can picture them when times get tough, even if they're not there. They can be our cheer-leaders and our rewards for each experiment. And we can reciprocate when they need to turn to us.

CREATIVE STRATEGIES

CALM PACKS
A calm pack is simply a portable pleasure zone. It contains anything you'd like to have with you as a support you when times get tough. It could be visual, sensory, intellectual, or a mixture. It could contain cards with affirming messages, a bottle of water, an apple and a stress ball. It could contain photographs of friends that you know are cheering you on as you take the next step to overcoming

your claustrophobia. It could be something someone has given or made for you, something to smell, taste or touch (Bombèr 2007).

The point is, *overcoming claustrophobia doesn't have to be grim*. Start associating time in confined spaces with pleasure and you're entering whole new realms of experience.

CREATIVE EXPRESSION

Painting, drawing or writing prose or poetry about your experiences of claustrophobia can be transformative. Art is a way of deepening our self-knowledge. It has been described as 'medicine' - acts of simple creative self-expression can be healing in so many ways. These modes of expression go beyond the verbal, providing the possibility of externalising your feelings, sensations and thoughts in a tangible, real-world form, rather than being bottled up - closed in - inside you.

The creative process may give you some release from tension and distress, and enable you to have a different perspective on what is happening for you, as well as creating a means of sharing what you experience with other people. Keeping your images or writing, subsequently making more and noticing how your experience changes over time can show you how far you've travelled, and draw attention to details you hadn't noticed that might need attention. You don't have to be 'good at art' or 'good at writing' to express yourself in these ways. Sincerity is all that's needed. The pictures, poems, or even models or music you make are what they are, perfect in themselves. Allow yourself to play, to be curious, to explore.

And of course you can use art and writing in many other ways. What is the opposite of claustrophobia for you? How about creating your own images and poems of light, freshness, resilience, freedom, joy? You might keep them in your calm pack (see above) or enjoy visualising them (see below) at a later date

DISTRACTION

"I distract myself by talking and listening to other people"

"I do normal things to take my mind off the tunnel when I take Eurostar, like reading and eating"

"I try to think of other things"

"I try to distract myself - close my eyes, listen to music, read, but it's not always successful"

"My lovely husband described a beautiful place we both know whilst I was having an MRI scan, it was a wonderful distraction"

There are many different views on whether distraction is a good idea. If you want to dispense with all your safety behaviours (*see* p. 208) then you may want to skip this list!

However, using distraction may help you get in the lift, go back on the train, enable you to stay in the back of the small car behind two huge passengers - which means that you will then have tangible evidence that you *can* manage that situation. You may have done it with the 'prop' of distraction, but it means that you've defeated that piece of avoidance. The knowledge that you've done it before may help you with your next experiment, which might well include going back to the space *without* the distraction, or with less of it. And of course distraction can make being in a confined space infinitely more pleasurable and interesting: boredom, after all, is a great seedbed for unhelpful frustration and worry.

In some situations, we may judge that becoming unaware of our surroundings through distraction is not a problem. Many people sleep on planes, for example, trusting that the crew are doing everything in their power to keep the plane safe. At other times, we decide we want to keep a generalised awareness of what's going on. The more we consider ourselves individually responsible for safety, the more likely we are to want to stay aware. It's a question of finding a personal balance that works for you. What will help you stop avoiding confined spaces? What will make you unhelpfully oblivious?

I READING

Identified by many as one of their favourite means of distraction from claustrophobic feelings, reading has the great advantage of being a readily available and portable means of transporting us from our present enclosed circumstances to another time, space and experience. Absorption in our books, magazines or newspapers can transform our feeling from anxiety to comfort and relaxation. Travelling, waiting for appointments or in any situation where you have to remain for a protracted period -going through a car-wash or in queues, for example - all provide time and space to read.

> Visualise yourself in the situation, relaxed, turning the pages
> of your favourite novel, taken up by a story in the paper,
> or solving that really challenging crossword, maybe even
> sorry that you're getting close to your destination or your
> appointment's time has come or the car-wash programme
> is over!

Such images run contrary to the disaster scenarios we can all too easily create when we envisage ourselves stuck in an enclosed space, so we are offering our brains an alternative possibility, associating a potentially anxiety-making situation with another, more constructive feeling.

Books carry positive connotations for many people, and we have access to these associations even if we don't open a page. Simply knowing that you have something to read with you can be of assistance, especially if you're contemplating a new challenge, perhaps going back on the tube after a long absence, or taking a lift. Books and papers can provide micro-steps away from your dependency on 'props' to enter or remain in the confined space which you fear.

So the reading-material-as-security blanket has many possibilities! apart from the genuine interest we may find in the contents. And of course we can find books that really make us laugh, with all the anti-anxiety benefits laughter brings (*see* section on laughter as anti-phobia therapy, p. 130).

MORE BOOK-BASED IDEAS

✓ Ask a friend or partner to lend you a book, and use a photo of him or her as a book-mark.

✓ Make your own book to carry with you, part of your calm-pack perhaps (see above). This could be a notebook or even ring-binder of encouraging comments from friends, inspiring pictures, thoughts and ideas that you find confidence-building and affirming, jokes you've heard, amusing things you've seen or that have happened to you. You could get a friend or a child to help you have fun making the book: the memory will come back each time you pick it up. In time, you may get to know the book so well that you can picture its contents in your mind's eye, giving you just as much pleasure and relaxation as the real thing.

✔   Bibliotherapy involves reading books recommended for help with any particular issue. In the Resources section on p. 256, you'll find a range of titles on themes covered in this book - there's bound to be something that speaks your language. And no harm in reading about overcoming fear when you're trying to do just that - just like taking a shopping list when you go shopping, in fact.

✔   If you find yourself without an actual book, there are plenty of other book-based ideas for distraction. Think of plots of books you've read already, books you could give specific friends or family as presents, books you wish you'd written, and all the books you could write, or indeed have written about you. Ask the people round you to tell you what their favourite book is, and why, what their favourite childhood book was, and why: start your own on-the-spot book club...

On the other hand... One of the disadvantages of reading as distraction on journeys is that the visual concentration required can induce motion sickness. I love reading on planes, and found it enormously helpful in reducing anxiety, but I've long since realised that trying to concentrate in turbulence isn't all that effective. Even when we're on solid ground, for example in a window-less hospital waiting room, unfortunately, if we're anxious and our hyper-vigilant eyes scan the pages too quickly, it can create a sensation of nausea. Simple cards with images or short, affirming messages (*see* Resources) might be helpful.

A second disadvantage may be the effects of the actual contents. It's unlikely that reading about someone stuck in a cave will do much to relieve your feelings of claustrophobia! - unless you're also reading about how that individual overcame the challenges, and used their strength and resilience to cope with the situation So that could well cut out some of the lengthier descriptions in *Northern Lights, Lord of the Rings,* or the script from *Panic Room,* for example. Similarly, if you are reading material that makes you feel in tune with characters who are vulnerable or emotionally strained, even if they are not in an enclosed space, your ordinary self-protective psychological boundaries may be compromised in an unhelpful way, as this man discovered:

"I had a panic attack in an MRI scan. Before the scan I was reading a book, whilst waiting, and was engrossed in the feelings it stirred up. I think my empathy/imaginative identification was on full power. I then unfortunately applied that same ability to what could happen to me whilst encased in plastic and felt awful!"

Thirdly, deep absorption in a book may make you less prepared if something potentially dangerous actually does occur. Although we probably keep our hearing sense active when we are reading, it won't be so acute if we are totally immersed. In this way, the 'safety behaviour' of reading can possibly make us vulnerable to an upsurge of panic, if the unexpected happens.

So, the trick is to find the books, magazines and newspapers that work for you, that enable you to be relaxed, empowered, but not necessarily too far removed from your reality.

2 SUDOKU AND OTHER NUMBER GAMES

The relatively new phenomenon of sudoku has been mentioned by many people as helpful. The game is based on a grid of nine nine-by-nine boxes, in which nine sequences of numbers from one to nine must be entered so that each horizontal and vertical line and each square of nine boxes only contains each number once.

There are three interesting benefits of sudoko as a distraction for people who experience claustrophobia. The first is that suduko is very portable, requiring only the grid and a pencil or pen (I have been known to ask strangers on planes and trains if I can copy their sudoku grid into my notebook - this has lead to interesting conversations, and no-one has ever minded). The second benefit is that sudoko is a numerical game of completely unassailable logic, with only one outcome, so there is no room for fantasy or the kind of word/image-based machinations often required by cryptic crosswords. So the challenge can help those of us who experience claustrophobia find focus, and come out of the imaginative world which may be fuelling our anxiety with '*What if...?*' disaster scenarios.

Thirdly, logic, reasoning, working with numbers and sorting is a frontal brain activity. If you actively put your 'executive' brain to work, emotional arousal tends to diminish. So sudoku can have a directly calming and containing effect on our anxieties.

On the other hand... Even people who love sudoku can sometimes feel it is a complete waste of time, if not life. Frustration arises when you get stuck, or you feel you've spent far too long focused on little boxes. Not the best idea for people who experience claustrophobia! Another problem is that we tend to sit very still whilst we're doing it. Whilst you're relaxed that's fine, but if tensions builds when the solution eludes you, or you're already feeling anxious, you're likely to feel fresher if you move around.

3 MUSIC AND OTHER AUDIO INPUT

The iPod is the latest variant of portable music systems which help people who experience claustrophobia. Not only can music give you anxiety-reducing pleasure and relaxation, it can have positive associations to people, experiences and places away from the confined space you are trying to tolerate. It can help your mind 'float', rather than become fixated on 'potential threats'. Rhythm can have a huge effect on feelings: Mozart, for example, has been shown to have positive mood-enhancing effects on brain waves, but then so can your favourite jazz or rock singer. In addition, music may make us move, which means our muscles are working and our circulation enhanced, with positive effects on well-being even in small, confined spaces. We can all work out what will soothe or stimulate us, and whether a lot of stimulation in an enclosed space makes us feel better or actually leaves us more frustrated because our desire to boogie conflicts with the seat-belt sign, or the demands of the radiographer operating the MRI scanner.

Other audio input includes podcasts, talking books, or study or relaxation tapes, so there is a vast choice. And just as books or magazines can be used as part of a moving away from safety behaviours, so can music and other audio material, by creating a step-by-step approach to experiencing the claustrophobic situation, and/or as reward for doing so.

Of course many people use music, radio and tapes in cars both for enjoyment and to reduce feelings of stuckness, especially in traffic jams, but elsewhere headphones can create quite a snug cocoon-like feeling, blocking out the world. This can help if, for example you don't want to hear the sound of the MRI scanner, fixate on the finer variations in a plane's engines, or notice when a train goes into a tunnel.

On the other hand... Being cut off from the 'real world', especially with headphones, can make sudden 're-entry' difficult. The shock effect can be heightened if something does happen, if you are suddenly dragged out of your reverie, and are less prepared to deal with whatever is happening than you might have been had you 'seen it coming'. This is another example of how a 'safety behaviour' can actually contribute to the very situation that the behaviour was intended to avert. So using music as distraction needs to be tempered with keeping an awareness of real world circumstances.

4 COMPUTERS AND ELECTRONIC GAMES
Much of what has been said above applies to computers and electronic games. They offer us wonderful distraction, enabling us to enter or stay in the kinds of spaces we fear, but equally can cause us to lose our awareness of our immediate circumstances.

A further consideration is the effects of computers on our brains, especially with wireless connection to the internet. The jury is still largely out on this, but what is obvious is that computers do reinforce our sense that real life should move at computer-like speed. So using electronic equipment as distraction could make us become more agitated than we might otherwise feel, adding to the sense of claustrophobia. It seems that different people have different tolerance for electronic equipment; if you're one of the fortunate ones, the possibilities of distraction are enormous.

FILMS AND TV - USING FANTASY CONSTRUCTIVELY
An article by Gary Susman on the Popwatch website (www.popwatch.ew.com) listed the "Most Claustrophobic Movies of All Time" (23rd Feb 2005). Here are some examples:

Flightplan, A Taste of Cherry, Das Boot, Papillon, Casino, Oxygen, Simon Magus, Panic Room) - and attracted further suggestions such as - *Contact,* the first *Die Hard, Diary of Ann Frank, The Hole, Cube, My Little Eye, The Poseidon Aventure, The Serpent and the Rainbow, The Shining, Rear Window, The Lady Vanishes, Marooned, Apollo 13, Towering Inferno, Dead Calm, The Collector, Sleuth, Repulsion, The Tenant, and Kill Bill 2* ... the list is long.

More generically, I would add any film or TV programme where people crawl up or down ducts, tunnels, sewers, or get stuck in lifts, cars, caves, coffins, cages, underwater or with water rising, (or indeed being locked in a lift underwater in a collapsing Venetian house, as in the most recent James Bond movie, just to up the tension a fraction!) or are imprisoned anywhere.

My sense is that people who can watch - and even enjoy - such films probably do not experience claustrophobia in real life. One contributor to the website wrote -

> "*The Uma* (Thurman*)-is-Buried-Alive scene of* 'Kill Bill 2' *was the most claustrophobic moment of my life".*

This person is *not* likely to be someone who panics at the prospect of using lifts or sitting in the back seat of a three-door car. The problem for those of us who experience claustrophobia is that having once seen such images, they can be hard to shift, and can affect us long after the film is finished. How does this occur?

WATCHING TV AND FILMS IS A VERY PASSIVE EXPERIENCE
Firstly, it can sometimes be hard to predict when claustrophobia-inducing moments are going to occur on screen. Obviously we can choose to avoid films and so on where the clue is in the title

or synopsis - *Cube, The Hole, Panic Room,* anything about being on an aeroplane or submarine - there's bound to be trouble! But elsewhere, such images can crop up very unexpectedly, perhaps, at worst, when we have been lulled into a false sense of security and are relatively relaxed. This gives us no time to look away or close our eyes, or at home, to hide behind cushions or the sofa (or larger members of our family).

Watching television is a very passive experience, far more so than reading - our brain wave patterns change and slow down. Stimulation from the screen means sensory input is reduced to seeing and hearing, so we are not physically prepared to protect ourselves. Just as in hypnosis, where the patient is relaxed in order to facilitate openness to suggestion, if we have no sense of what is coming, we may be vulnerable to images that affect us deeply. Information and images enter unfiltered, directly into the memory, without analysis*. I hesitate to use the word traumatising, but powerful images can certainly stimulate the beating heart, racing pulse, sickened stomach and dry mouth associated with fear and panic states, re-activated later if we continue to think about the images or find them hard to push out of our minds.

Films and television programmes give us ideas and images which sensitise us to environmental possibilities that would not have occurred to us before. Repeated exposure may turn possibilities into spurious probabilities. Just as, for example, anyone watching the *Inspector Morse* series over the years might well get the impression that living in Oxford is far more dangerous than it actually is. Or that the cities in which *CSI* teams operate have a high concentration of murderers capable of the most extraordinary ingenuity.

Our sense of the world as a dangerous place and the *likelihood*

*Levine, *Commonsense Rebellion (Continuum, 2001)*

of such events occurring can undoubtedly be increased by such exposure. Can our brains distinguish between fantasy and reality if our nightly visual 'body count' is so high? Of course this is the skill of the film or programme-maker, to create strong images that move people. We are much more likely to feel and to respond empathically if we see something awful happening to someone than if we simply hear about it. News broadcasts and charity appeals on television showing images of great human suffering and need in tsunami or earthquake or famine affected countries, depend on this truth.

Empathy is based on the ability to project oneself into the shoes of another, and to taste, even faintly, something of what that other person may be experiencing. When we switch from the news to an action movie, the deep and ancient parts of our brains may not be able to discriminate where our empathy should flow - between reality and fantasy - and our bodies react in a similar way - hence the beating heart and sweating palms.

Perhaps this is most true for people with highly developed imaginations, strong empathy and rich inner worlds. Of course it is possible to say to oneself - *"This man is not really stuck in a lift in a building which is on fire, he's an actor on a film-set surrounded by a crew"* - when a film or programme has a strongly negative effect on us. However, the neural circuits of brains which have registered the visual trigger of *'lift-in-tall-building'* = *'cause-for-alarm'* may have been activated at a deep physiological level.

The challenge then is how to make reassuring words and thoughts reach this level of arousal. Many people who experience claustrophobia find that words are not enough, or that the connection between these rational thoughts and our feelings is not strong enough to be effective. We need to find additional forms of reassurance, such as touch, visualisation, and particular tones of voice (*see above, in Voice*.) to make the words and thoughts more genuinely soothing to ourselves. And we need to learn to distinguish between experiencing empathy for real distress (helpful) and empathy aroused by fiction (not helpful). We don't want to lose the helpful, human aspects of our capacity to 'feel into' someone else's experience. We simply want to lose the downside, or at least diminish its impact.

✔   Don't watch films or programmes with giveaway titles or synopses!

✔   If you have been upset or agitated as a result of watching something, move around to disperse the build-up of adrenaline. Push down and really feel your feet on the floor, or push against a wall with your hands. Stroke down your arms and legs with strong, slow, powerful strokes, telling the image to go away and get out of your system. Shout at it if necessary. Tell it it's just fiction. Blow out hard. Stamp. Shake your shoulders. Dance around the kitchen. Fill your body with strong energy. Feel powerful and say "*Yes*" to your power.

✔   Look around your real environment, name and touch what you see: for example - "*There is a black hob, a white fridge, some green and lilac curtains, a row of coffee mugs*". Become more specific the more anxious you feel: "*The mugs are lime green, dark green, mauve and white, and sandy-coloured, and they are on the mug-stand. My favourite is the patchwork Italian china mug. It feels smooth and cool.*" Actively noticing what is real and tangible 'grounds' us in our present experience.

✔   Get angry as a way of "fighting" the fearful feelings. Angry that you were frightened unnecessarily. Angry that there is distress in the world, angry about global warming, angry about the price of cheese, angry that something supposed to entertain you actually makes you feel bad - it doesn't matter what, just find the strength in anger rather than allowing yourself to feel the victim of the imagery.

✔ If you feel able to re-visit the image that has frightened you, picture all the people alongside the actors - the director, producer, camera-crew. Imagine everyone on set supporting the main actor, who may well be feeling claustrophobic themselves. Douglas Hensall and Christopher Lee have both acknowledged experiences of claustrophobia in their work as actors, as has Anthony Daniels, who played C-3PO in Star Wars*. Picture your favourite actor feeling reassured, and going on to perform brilliantly, as these actors do.

✔ If you are confident that you can do the above to dispel the feelings, then you could use the opportunity to stay in the situation to build some tolerance of anxiety, as a practice for when you may experience anxiety in an enclosed space, or if you got trapped. Think about the kind of training the stunt people may have had. Build your capacity to think whilst you are anxious, to notice, discern, make decisions. Use your power.

FREEDOM

Experiencing claustrophobia is to fear being trapped. It makes sense, therefore, to try to maximise our freedom whenever we're *not* in a confined place. To make the most of the privileges and

* personal communication

pleasures of freely moving our bodies, dancing, running, cycling, stretching, exerting ourselves: travelling, swimming in the wide open sea, standing on mountains, enjoying huge expansive vistas, sunshine, moonlight, fresh air: talking, singing, laughing, arguing, hugging, playing, making love ...

If we spend the vast majority of our days alone and indoors, our claustrophobia may simply be an extension of cabin fever.

MINDFULNESS

Mindfulness is a practice of paying attention to the present moment, being fully conscious of everything happening inside and outside ourselves. It has been compared to meditation, but is not necessarily used for any kind of spiritual reason.

It is a process of paying attention -

✔ to what is happening in our surrounding environment - the sounds, sights, smells and so on

✔ to our bodies (through body 'scanning', feeling each part from the inside, or by focusing on our breath)

✔ to our feelings, without judging what we find, or trying to change anything

✔ to our thoughts, whether they be about what we have noticed in our bodies or in our environment, or about something completely different. We can allow our thoughts to come and go, as if we were sitting on a river bank, watching each thought float downstream like leaves.

Mindfulness can be experienced as a neutral receptive state, or we can allow ourselves to feel love and compassion towards everything we notice.

There are several benefits of practising mindfulness for people who experience claustrophobia. It brings us fully into the present, enabling us to notice what is *actually* happening rather than what we might *imagine* is happening or is *about to* happen. It develops our ability to concentrate, to slow down, relax and de-stress, and to regard our circumstances calmly. It enables us to notice our internal state and our environment, so we are alert to changes, and can respond appropriately, but because we're not extrapolating from what we notice, we're less likely to catastrophise. Mindfulness may help us build our 'internal witness', the third part of ourselves that can mediate between our logical self and our feelings self, rather than one unhelpfully dominating the other (*see* p. 101).

RESILIENCE

In claustrophobia, we have an opportunity to develop our resilience. To be resilient has a wonderful ring to it. It has echoes of resistance, immunity, tenacity, determination, robustness, and positivity; of tempered metal, of those round-bottomed Japanese dolls that right themselves no matter how many times they are knocked over. It speaks more of thriving than simply surviving, of being engaged in life rather than hiding from obstacles and setbacks. Developing resilience can strengthen our capacity to take on claustrophobia, amongst much else.

There seem to be five key qualities and capacities that resilient people repeatedly demonstrate. We may know we have strengths in some aspects, but want to develop others. Resilient people -

✔ have a sense of belonging. They feel attached to significant other people in their lives, and to the wider community. They feel compassion and respect for others, value connection and mutual exchange, and can ask for and give support. They don't try to do everything alone.

✓ They see themselves as responsible for their lives. They have confidence in their own judgement. They focus on priorities and strengths, and take opportunities. They can be flexible and adaptable.

✓ They have a learning, information-seeking approach to problem-solving, and are willing to put in effort and determination to succeed. They trust their body-based instincts as well as being open to input from others. They have high emotional intelligence.

✓ They are secure in their bodies and feelings, and have a strong sense of pleasure and joy. They use humour.

✓ They believe life has meaning. They believe in having a role and making a contribution; that what we do as individuals matters. They feel connected to the earth and natural beauty.

All of us can build our strengths in any of these areas.

At a quick glance, in which area do you feel most confident? How have you developed this area? What would continue the process?

Which area do you get the sense needs strengthening, when you think about your experiences of claustrophobia?

What could be a first step towards doing this? What support could you find to do this? What would help make the process enjoyable?

Brian Keenan is an outstanding example of a resilient person dealing with a situation of total entrapment. Keenan was kidnapped in Beirut in the 80's, and spent four and a half years in captivity, often in solitary confinement, mostly in very small, dark or totally unlit rooms. His inspiring book, *An Evil Cradling* (Vintage, 1993) can be very hard to read, especially for those people who already experience claustrophobia and who make the empathic leap to the circumstances in which he was held prisoner.

Nonetheless, this powerful book has many fine lessons for us on how to handle a situation of being trapped, albeit in very different, brief and far more mundane circumstances. Keenan experienced profound claustrophobia on many occasions throughout his imprisonment. He learned that his anxiety followed certain patterns, and found ways of managing, including taking up the role of his 'own self-observer': He was thrown back on his own resources time and again, and devised many inventive ways for maintaining his stability, mental and physical well-being whilst confined. The qualities of resilient people listed above were never so clearly demonstrated.

REWARDS, CELEBRATION AND THE CONTRIBUTION WE CAN MAKE

No-one is going to give us a medal the first time we lock the loo door, go into the far corner of the cupboard-under-the-stairs to get that old pair of trainers or manage late-night shopping crowds in a busy department store. But if you're someone who has experienced claustrophobia, you'll know what an achievement these simple acts represent. Achievements need to be celebrated and rewarded - think of yourself as a Formula One driver, ready for champagne!

As humans, we're all receptive to reward. Anticipating

something pleasurable or celebratory can be the motivating factor that pulls us through the next step of challenging our claustrophobia, whether it be as simple as a coffee, glass of wine, chocolate, new book, a walk in the countryside, or as significant as finding a more rewarding job, returning to work we love, meeting up with friends and family, or travelling to places we've always wanted to go.

When we think of a reward to encourage ourselves to take the next step, it's essential we 'follow through', and actually give ourselves that thing or experience, once we've accomplished our aim. As I've mentioned elesewhere (p. 121), building trust between different aspects of ourselves is an essential part of recovery from claustrophobia. Our scared 'self' needs to know that our encouraging 'self' means what he or she says. Real world rewards mean a lot to our psyche, especially if they make us happy.

We can use the image of the thing we're looking forward to to sustain us whilst we're in the confined space, as much as at the planning stage. And we can reward each tiny step we make as well, not just the big things. Each new effort and experiment represents rejection of the voice of fear, a triumph for our growing strength, courage and determination, a victory for our willingness to grow in resilience. There can also be reward in knowing that each individual act of overcoming our own fears makes a contribution to the health and well-being of everyone else. This may seem a grand claim, but consider.

Firstly, as people with a keen sense of our environment, we can draw attention to aspects of confined spaces that are genuinely dangerous or unnecessarily uncomfortable and potentially traumatising, as I describe in Chapter 6. We can encourage everyone involved in the design of spaces that hold people to find solutions that prioritise human needs and preferences.

Secondly, when we trust we can deal with what's happening

for us, we can look outside ourselves, notice what other people need, share our strength and experience. When we're scared and limited because of our fear, we're less in a position to be generous and encouraging and supportive of other people.

Buddhist writers such as William Bloom and Thich Nhat Hanh gently remind us that safety is not an individual matter. Everything we achieve as an individual, in the direction of feeling secure, calm, in touch with kindness and compassion, will benefit our community. How we sit, speak and walk can show the other person he or she is safe (or not). In a panic situation, one person able to calm themselves makes a huge difference. And helping other people feel safe guarantees one's own safety. What we do matters.

Thirdly, telling our story can help - letting others people know about our vulnerablility and our journey towards getting stronger, can embolden them to face their own difficulties. The stories I read from the contributors to this book emboldened me, as did reading accounts like *An Evil Cradling* by Brian Keenan (Vintage 1993), and *Out of the Tunnel*, by Rachel North (Friday Books, 2007). Sharing our stories is like calling out to each other as we each climb the same mountain - I may not be able to see you, round the other side of that rock, but hearing your voice and replying from my own stretch of the track reminds both of us that we are not alone. Calmness and confidence can be contagious.

And not only for others who've struggled with claustrophobia. When I went back on the underground the first time, my step-daughter called from New Zealand with congratulations. She has no problems with confined spaces. Her 'thing' is spiders: many's the time I was summoned to remove them for her when she shared our house in London. She compared my return to travelling by tube to her sitting beside a tarantula. *"I know what terror feels like,"* she said, *"and I really admire what you've done"*. Recently she emailed to say that she'd managed to spend the night in the same room as a spider, major progress for her. And her success, and care in sharing appreciation motivated me further, a positive spiral of encouragement.

Claustrophobia is a major challenge in our lives, and an opportunity to become stronger, more supportive people. Each step of overcoming it is cause for celebration.

ROLES

"Talking to people - I walked seventy-seven steps down a tight spiral staircase telling a nervous child behind me what was coming next round each bend. It really helped. Focusing on making it easier for her really calmed my own anxiety, gave me a role".

In times of high stress and tension, it may be that having *a role* protects us from the trauma of the situation. Training enables emergency service staff to remain calm in situations that most people find terrifying, *to 'keep their heads...'*, continuing to think and act appropriately. Their approach is not really one of stoicism, more one of an automatic sense of *'getting on with the job'*. It may be that once their professional minds are not so focused on the task in hand, that emotions stirred up by the situation can be felt. Staff may then need support to let go and deal with their distress, just like any 'civilian'.

In numerous emergency situations, ordinary people have found their own way to calmness by talking to and helping other people, drawing on the basic need to connect as well as offering first-aid skills. Some become instant reporters, taking mobile phone photographs to send to the press. Still others mobilise their sense of humour and become comedians. If we had to deal with being stuck in a confined space, what might our roles be, to see us through?

Our role, in minor or major situations of being trapped or stuck, does not have to be a particular job. It could be connected to a quality you enjoy expressing - gentleness, curiosity, defiance. It could be an aspect of identity, like Liverpudlian, Londoner, party lover, good neighbour, peace-maker, explorer. Perhaps it's no co-incidence that cognitive behaviour therapists, themselves highly trained in research methods, encourage their clients to take the role of researchers into their own behaviour, by noticing their reactions in the avoided situation. In *An Evil Cradling* former hostage Brian Keenan repeatedly refers to drawing strength from his core identity as a (bearded) Irishman. He experienced a huge range of emotions in his time as a hostage; but this deep part of his identity was the one that repeatedly enabled him to regard what happened to him as an injustice to be resisted.

In whatever we love being and doing, we can find the seeds of the 'role' we can adopt if we find ourselves confined

VISUALISATION

The ability to be able to create vivid internal images in our mind's eye is a wonderful thing, *if*, and it's a huge **IF**, the images we create enrich, nourish and delight us, rather than create terror and distress (see *Films*, above). Visualisation may be primarily visual, but can also include physical sensation, sound, even impressions of taste and smell. Visualisation may be used in hypnotherapy (*see* p. 230), to 'plant' positive images into the unconscious mind when the patient is in a deep state of relaxation. Look at the list of places and situations in which people who experience claustrophobia feel happy and relaxed, on p. 44. How much time do you spend visualising such situations? How do you feel when you let yourself do this? Could you do it more often?

My sense is that as people who experience claustrophobia, we are often very good at visualising, but need to learn to de-activate the intensity of painful images and work at creating beneficial ones. If we've been traumatised, we may experience flashbacks, the image of the traumatic incident being played and re-played in our psyches, sometimes as a result of a trigger reminding us of the initial incident, sometimes out-of-the-blue. Techniques such as EMDR (*see* p. 228) and Hypnotherapy (*see* p. 230) have proved effective in helping to dis-empower the intensity of this experience, to 'un-couple' or disconnect the association the brain has made between the memory of the confined space and our emotional response to it (of anxiety).

We can actively use visualisation to change the memory of a trauma. We can visualise our support network (*see above, and* p. 19), even if the people involved were not actually with us at the time. We can 'watch' them in our mind's eye like giants, standing between us and the oncoming vehicle that crashed into our car, pushing it back with super-human strength. Watch them wrench the doors of the walk-in fridge open, knock down the chef who thought it was a joke to lock us in, and then see us all running out into the warm sunshine, shouting with pride. Watch ourselves handling that MRI scan completely differently - asking for and getting the support we should have been given, having our friends in the room, dancing to the music we love, settling into the process feeling calm and capable. The more vividly we can create these new scenarios, the more the brain will have other associations to hand when anxiety is triggered again.

Even if there hasn't been a specific incident of trauma, we can still use this process to counter threatening imagery we may have when thinking about confined spaces. Some people may find it helpful to visualise the worst-case scenario, what they really fear may happen to them in confined spaces, and then, how they'd deal with what happened.   To think this thought can be unbearable, and yet some people find relief doing this: anything else they experience might subsequently seem like a lesser issue.

We can use visualisation at every stage of overcoming claustrophobia. At the planning stage, picturing ourselves going through the whole experience with confidence and relaxation, emerging proud and happy afterwards; during the time in the confined space, whether we pass through, or get stuck. We can picture our support network, imagine their presence in the situation with us and even have conversations with them. We can visualise our secure base (*see above*) and run to it in our imagination from wherever we are. Once we get there, we can visualise our calm, our relief, our pleasure at being safe, and flood our systems with chemicals of peace and relaxation.

Finally, we can enjoy visualising what life might be like beyond claustrophobia! Now that really *is* a picture...

Chapter 9

Confined spaces re-visited;
lifts, MRI scanners, the underground and other forms of transport

This section explores some of the specific situations that people who experience claustrophobia identify as problematic: enclosed spaces designed by humans to 'hold humans' - lifts, MRI scanners, the tube (London Underground), trains, and other kinds of transport.

Each context presents its own particular challenges. Each has elements of design and function that can be improved, where 'superior' solutions of benefit to people who experience claustrophobia would be or are of benefit to everyone. And there are particular strategies that I and many others have found helpful in overcoming claustrophobic anxiety in each situation.

LIFTS

Lifts are frequently cited as problematic by people who experience claustrophobia. Lifts are one of the most confined places that we voluntarily go into as humans, so it's not surprising that they should be such a trigger for claustrophobia.

There are millions and millions of lift journeys taken every day. Only a tiny fraction of these journeys result in lifts getting stuck, and an even tinier fraction result in anyone being hurt or injured. But still the small space we see as the door opens can trigger memories of other difficult experiences, and induce panic quite quickly.

When my claustrophobia was at its peak, I felt too terrified to use them at all. Gradually, over time, I became capable of being in a lift with family or close friends, but not if there were other people around. My husband became expert at lift stories. A lift story is a tale you quickly invent to keep your wife's or friend's minds off the fact that they are in a lift, and continue as long as it takes to travel the requisite number of floors. Some lift stories are as short as haiku: others have casts of characters worthy of Dickens.

Lifts are one of the spaces people would most like to be able to use again, recognising that not being able to do so can affect travel, work possibilities, socialising and many other aspects of life. After all, lifts have changed the way we live. In 2007, Otis, the world's oldest - and largest - lift manufacturer, celebrated 150 years since the first lifts, as we know them today, began to travel. Without lifts we wouldn't have skyscrapers, blocks of flats or other high buildings, or indeed deep mines. Our environment has been fundamentally changed by their invention.

Lift technology has become highly developed, with safety prioritised both in terms of operation and breakdown assistance. Otis, for example, services more than a million lifts worldwide, and as with all lift manufacturers, incorporates a huge range of safety features, including 'remote monitoring'. This system detects faults, and will automatically dial Otis to inform the company of the lift location, the nature of the problem and whether anyone is trapped. An engineer can be dispatched, and the people inside the lift spoken with directly. Emergency lighting is provided in many modern lifts, along with procedures that kick in once the alarm is pressed, so that you'd still be helped even if you couldn't speak or speak a foreign language. If a lift is in a building where there's not likely to be someone on site to hear an alarm, then the UK Health & Safety Executive recommends the installation of a telephone in the lift itself.

Points to consider on returning to lifts

1   Choose your lift! - clearly not all lifts are as well constructed as others. There's no point in putting yourself in a creaky old lift with slow-closing doors for your first experiment - give yourself the best chance of succeeding and not being re-traumatised. Part of your experimenting can be getting to know different kinds of lifts, perhaps from the outside at the beginning, before you venture inside. People who experience claustrophobia often find that lifts with mirrors work well, both because they increase the sense of space and because you can look at yourself. If you see your face is anxious, or your shoulders hunched, you can consciously relax, which will have powerful calming effects on the rest of your body and psyche. A lift in a public place is probably preferable for first experiments than a rarely used one, for example, in an unattended multi-storey carpark at the weekend. A lift in a shop or a large, well-used hotel has to be kept in good repair, and if there were to be a break-down, there would be many people around to help. Choose whether you want your experiment to include travelling with other people, or just you and a buddy (p. 143).

2   Lifts travelling long distances often go faster than ones which stop at every floor. Watch the lights that indicate how long it usually takes to go the number of floors you want, and hold onto the knowledge that your journey is likely to only take a similar amount of time. Remember you can build back up to journeys of several floors - you may want to start simply by going one floor, and then walking the rest of the way. Better for your health, in any case!- and a great way to burn off any feelings aroused by your experience.

3   Find out what works for you, in terms of where you place your attention. Would you rather watch the doors close or look at the floor? Would you rather watch the floor numbers appear or listen to the sound the lift makes in the shaft? Would you like a corner view or to stand near the front? Is it better to put your weight onto one foot, or balance it evenly? Notice your surroundings. What kind of lift is it? Who is the manufacturer? What kind of safety instructions are there? How could this lift be improved? What suggestions would you make to management? Allowing yourself to notice and be discriminating about what you observe and how you observe it can help arouse the reflective, discerning part of your brain, enabling the more emotional part to relax and know that all is well.

4   Choose your companions. Take a buddy with you, to experiment with using lifts, with either just the two of you alone in the lift or the two of you plus other lift-users as well, whatever you want to try as your next challenge. Agree in advance whether you want to be distracted with chat or to focus on your experience. If it's just the two of you, you can use your voices however you want. Recite poetry. Tell jokes and stories. Use the lift as your private karaoke booth. Go in full evening dress or a jogging suit. Go in role as your favourite film stars or rock idols. Find out what works for you.

Whatever you do, however you manage the journey, you're building up a memory bank of having done it before, and surviving. This means a huge amount to your psyche, which hitherto was being alarmed with ideas that the danger of lifts was so immense there could only be one (very gloomy) outcome. Now it has new evidence to help reduce the conviction that getting stuck is inevitable.

The lift game

As a way of planning going back to using lifts, you might try playing the lift game with friends - simply a matter of answering the question -

> Who would you most like to be stuck in a lift with?
>
> Some people might find it hard to even think about this, but if you can bring yourself to do so, you might find some interesting and helpful ideas, for three reasons. In the unlikely event that you were ever trapped, you could visualise the people you thought of. Secondly, your answers may give you information about what you need when you feel stuck, in lifts or anywhere else. And thirdly, it's a rather lateral way to acclimatise yourself to even thinking about lifts, an alternative to catastrophic imagery.
>
> *My current fellow trap-ees would include my immediate family (positive, practical, optimistic, funny, endless conversations): friends I never have enough time with: Nelson Mandela, so I could ask everything I've ever wanted to know about his view of life (and whose experience in small enclosed spaces would be helpful); George Clooney, definitely, Daniel Craig in best James Bond mode (though probably not in the same lift as my family) ... The list is getting long and my lift is getting full ...*
>
> So what does it show me I need? Human warmth - touch - communication - laughter - a sense of perspective - something to think about - lots of different kinds of contact ... I could work on that little list if I ever got stuck.

This is a good game to play with friends or family. Not only are their answers likely to be amusing (and revealing! - in one particular gathering where I asked this question, someone said *"a lift engineer"* - which left those of us who'd come up with a variety of screen gods and goddesses distinctly speechless), but it could be a safe way to introduce the idea that you experience claustrophobia to people who care about you.

IF THE LIFT DOES BREAKS DOWN …

In the vast majority of cases, being stuck in a lift is an inconvenience, and not a danger at all. The best possible thing to do is to wait for assistance once you've pressed the alarm, and know that help is on its way. Trying to escape is more likely to cause problems or injuries than waiting. It's important to know that specialist staff will be needed to help you leave the lift safely, and these may not be the people who first respond to your signal. Although everyone will be doing their best to get you out as quickly as possible, government directions require that safety is prioritised over speed. Knowing that the time being taken is actually to protect you may help you cope with the wait.

So it then becomes a question of taking care of yourself, as in any other situation of being stuck.

- ✓ Relaxation (p. 116) and breath steadying (p. 109)
- ✓ Mindfulness techniques (p. 164)
- ✓ Talking with other people, if there are any
- ✓ Distraction (p. 151)
- ✓ Thinking about your secure base (p. 148) and support network (p. 148), all the circles of support and care around you
- ✓ Chatting to the characters you conjured up in the lift game (*see above*)

✓   Re-creating past positive experiences, or coming up with ideal presents for friends

✓   Thinking ahead to people you'll see later, planning something you can look forward to in great detail

✓   Picturing your lift, and then in your mind's eye panning back to the building in the street in a town in a county in a huge landscape, which is fresh and open and full of light and air

✓   Using your imagination and your memory and your ability to self-soothe as the loving friends and allies they actually are

A final thought. Liz Hayward, poet, once said that she'd love to be stuck in a lift: she felt that it would give her a welcome and relaxing break from the demands of her family and work. What wouldn't you give to get some free time in your own busy life? If you could re-frame getting stuck in a lift as a chance to do just that, the possibility might even begin to look a bit inviting …

MRI SCANNERS

Many people who experience claustrophobia find the prospect of having to go for an MRI scan very daunting. Having to lie flat in a narrow enclosed tunnel, with limited vision and incapable of movement for the duration of the test, can create panic and distress. And mention to colleagues, friends or hairdresser that you have to have a scan and you are likely to be regaled with horror stories.

"My friend got stuck"

"The top of it is only an inch above your nose"

"They strapped me in and I started screaming before I even went in the scanner!"

Hardly very encouraging! Especially if you are, rather naturally, also worried about the symptoms that lead you to go to your GP in the first place. You certainly would not be alone - research suggests that between five and fifteen percent of patients refuse the procedure, and also suggests that the experience itself has actually triggered claustrophobia for the first time in some patients.

So the great news for people who are anxious about undergoing a conventional MRI scan is that you can now be referred to either of two excellent facilities in the UK that offer genuine alternatives: the Open MRI at the Nuffield Orthopædic Centre in Oxford, and the Upright MRI Centre in London (*see* Resources).

To picture being scanned by the Open MRI, imagine lying on a circular dais, in a large, well-lit room, with soft lights, music to your taste, and a calm voice over the intercom telling you you're doing brilliantly just for lying there. Sounds too good to be true? Only a little - the sole detail I have omitted is the presence of the other half of the scanner, which is suspended above you from the ceiling. The staff are behind a screen, in another room, but as with all other scanning facilities, you can have a friend or family member in the room with you if you like. For some scans, only a limited part of your body would need to be in the 'bun'; for others, a 'cage' may be used, partly round the head, for example, but it doesn't restrict vision that much. The arrangement of the scanner could give surgeons unique access to operate whilst the patient is in the scanner, reducing the need to call the patient back into hospital on a separate occasion.

The Upright MRI Centre in London is the first of its kind in the UK available (there is a research model in Aberdeen). It has been specifically developed with claustrophobic patients in mind, and has helpful information and pictures of the scanner on its website.

Dr. Ben Timmis, the Joint Medical Director of the Upright MRI Centre comments that there are three key components to providing excellence in his service. State-of-the art equipment, managed by very experienced radiography staff: expert clinicians who can accurately interpret the data the scanners provide: and calm, empathic, highly-trained 'front-of-house' staff, who are the first line of contact with patients - on the telephone, and then face-to-face on the unit - who can make all the difference in relaxing and reassuring people who are anxious about what the experience might involve.

To be scanned in the Upright MRI, the patient usually sits on a seat, facing forward, wearing a light seat-belt: the seat will be slightly retracted into the scanning equipment behind the chair and to both sides. The scanner is completely open above the head and in front. This position is very good for people who experience claustrophobia - it's far easier to have a sense of being in control when you are upright than if you are lying flat. The patient can easily see and communicate with the radiography staff on the other side of the screen, but may prefer to watch their own DVD on a plasma screen, or listen to music (remember to take a film set in the open countryside, and not a disaster movie!). At the end of the scan, you can simply walk out.

The health professionals at both the NOC and the Upright MRI Centre are friendly, responsive, and reassuringly matter-of-fact. They radiate good humour; are obviously genuinely interested to go out of their way to make the experience of being scanned as comfortable and easy as possible. They highlight the importance their teams place on helping people who experience claustrophobia to relax, and to feel in control at every stage in the process. This may include giving them a little extra time, which proves very effective. *"After all"*, says Stuart Wilson, senior radiographer at the NOC, *"when people come into hospital for tests, sense and sensibility fly out of the window. We understand that people are anxious. Whatever the patient can manage, is better than nothing. If we get even one scan, that's helpful"*.

Any disadvantages to these alternatives to conventional MRIs? Because of their configuration, Upright and Open MIR scans can take somewhat longer than a conventional scan to obtain data of completely comparable quality, so if you are of the grit-your-teeth-and-it-will-be-over-sooner school of thought, you may wish to go the traditional route. Scans at both centres are more costly than at conventional units, so you may have to argue for it. It's worth pointing out that a problem scanned early will give you the best chance of treatment and thus recovery, undoubtedly more cost effective long-term than leaving the problem un-addressed. Your experience of claustrophobia shouldn't undermine your right to the most appropriate assessment procedure, and the most sensitive care.

Is it possible to have a conventional scan, if you experience claustrophobia? Certainly. Today's conventional scanners are usually open at both ends, in the centre of an open room, and the size of the scanner bore has been increased. The ends are often flared, to give an impression of extra width. Where possible, the patient is not inserted headfirst. Noise has been reduced, and headphones are available to keep out the remainder. Angled mirrors are sometimes provided so that you can see the staff, and you can always communicate with them using an emergency buzzer. They are able to talk to you throughout the procedure.

But if you experience claustrophobia, and you need to go for a scan, it is worth remembering that these two excellent alternative facilities exist. Development of the new Open and

Upright MRI scanners shows that when health professionals really do listen to their patients, procedures and treatments can become more humane, and less stressful, for everyone involved. The MRI experience can be re-framed from being a stressful endurance test, to an opportunity to receive all the marvellous health-enhancing benefits this procedure offers. *

USING THE UNDERGROUND

The Underground or 'tube' train in London is mentioned frequently by people who experience claustrophobia as a form of transport they hate, only use if they have to or choose to avoid completely. Very few regard it with fondness. This isn't too surprising, even though the whole underground system is much cleaner and brighter than it used to be, as I discovered when I went back for the first time eight years after my scare in the Eurostar tunnel. But it's a huge part of London life, and being able to access it can be a great liberation for people who experience claustrophobia, opening up the city for pleasure and work. And if you can travel by underground in London, there's parts of the Tyne & Wear Metro, the Paris Metro, the New York subway, and even Tokyo to look forward to … but probably not for 'beginners'!

Perhaps the key point to remember in contemplating travelling by tube or subway is that much of our 'claustrophobic' response to and rejection of the limitations of the system is rational, extremely human, and shared by many others who use it but don't particularly enjoy doing so. Logically, if space, light, freedom of movement and fresh air are things you value, as most of us do, you're not going to find too much of them underground. To get to the trains, it's

* *With thanks to Gill Thomas, hypnotherapist, London.*

often necessary to go down long escalators, in busy lifts or down winding labyrinthine passageways. Even though our tube trains are not packed to Tokyo standards, they can still be very full of people pressed close together (the Japanese have methods of getting people to 'move down the carriage' we haven't even dreamt of). It can get very hot, and feel airless, especially when platforms are full, or when the train stops in a tunnel, because the air in the underground is largely moved by the trains themselves (the warmest lines are the Central and Bakerloo, according to London Underground, and the coolest are the District, Circle and most recently opened sections of the Jubilee Line). For this reason, London Underground is working on many new initiatives - groundwater cooling, ventilation fans, mechanical chillers - to bring fresher, cooler air into the system.

At least we have windows in the carriages, some of which even open a little. As I mentioned earlier, the first carriages on the City and South London line had none, because the manufacturers thought there was no point, with nothing to see in the tunnels. These carriages quickly acquired the nickname 'padded cells': the travelling public voted with their feet, and stayed away. Better designs followed!

With all that over-intimate body contact, there's almost an unspoken agreement amongst commuters that no-one speaks to each other. Rachel North, who survived the tube bombings in July 2005 describes this as the *"Don't Talk We're Londoners"* rule of London Tube travelling (*and see below*). The comedian Jason Bryne suggests that Londoners develop new ways of bending their necks, so that at all costs, they can avoid eye-contact with each other. So despite the noise of the brakes, and the sound of the train whipping through the tunnels, and despite all those people crammed in together, it can be a quiet and alienating experience. As passengers, we are dependent on the driver to communicate with us to tell us what is happening, and we each depend on all the other strangers in the carriage to behave with respect and restraint towards one another. And largely, that's what happens.

But humans are not worms, or peas to be processed, or lumps of coal to be whizzed on conveyor belts through subterranean passages, nor poor crated chickens, who weren't 'designed' for such confinement either. To travel on a crowded tube train requires us to move into a particular 'zone', which is not a particularly human state, if to be human is to move freely, to be spontaneous, to breathe deeply. It can require massive self-discipline, stoicism, tolerance of discomfort, compliance, and an almost Zen meditation-like detachment from our bodies.

Not many of us have those qualities readily to hand! Nor are they generally desirable - dissociation or detachment won't necessarily enable you to respond appropriately in an incident or accident. Those of us who experience claustrophobia have the mixed blessing of a keen sense of our environment, and an attunement to possible danger, and our bodies are often already 'primed' with adrenaline. We notice aspects of the system that others only become aware of 'after the event'. So if 'something' does happen, at least we may be ready for it. Detachment from our environment is absolutely not what 'overcoming claustrophobia' is all about.

Where our sensitivities let us down, however, is in our over-estimation of danger, our lack of confidence in our ability to tolerate fear, and our difficulty in believing that we could, if we had to, find a way to cope. And that is where our phobia kicks in, and we avoid what is an admittedly not always pleasant, but actually a very helpful, method of transport.

But you may have reached the decision that you would like to be able to travel by underground, for work, to visit friends or family, or for leisure. At its best, the tube is an extremely effective way of travelling through London and other cities, cutting journey time considerably, and is remarkably safe. The system carries around a billion people per year, with only one fatality for every 300 million journeys (The Economist 23rd October 2003).

Or course it is impossible to write about safe travelling on the London Underground without remembering those who died and were injured in the terrorist attacks of July 2005. The response to the bombings was very mixed, with some people feeling that this event marked an absolute end to their tube-taking career - *"always hated that crowded and trapped underground feeling"*, wrote one online contributor in the aftermath: *"rather be a live wimp than a dead hero"* wrote another. The numbers travelling by tube dropped in the immediate aftermath, before climbing back again. Many, however, were determined *"not to let the terrorists win"*, and either went back on the tube immediately or worked their way back gradually. Others had no choice; they had to get to work, and the tube was the only way. Some of the people who had been on the Piccadilly line train formed 'King's Cross United', a group that meets socially for solidarity, and campaigns for an enquiry; members support and celebrate each other's return to the Underground.

When she was thinking about going back on the Underground, Rachel North, one of the passengers on that train who subsequently wrote an extremely moving book about her experiences, realised that she had a choice. She could either view her fellow passengers as potential terrorists, or she could see them differently. She was determined not to contribute to making her beloved London into a *"paranoid, suspicious and angry place'*, but rather to *'celebrate how great being alive is in this diverse and beautiful and proud city"*.

"I try not to look at them (other people on the underground) as potential threats. I try to look at them as potential fellow passengers."

She could imagine that when she was on the tube, she'd be thinking about the bomb, *'the bang, smoke, screams'* - or she could think -

> *"... whether the face opposite me would be that face that looked into my eyes and held my hand if the unimaginable happened again. Or whether the stranger on the train would be the guide in the panic and the voice in the dark. If these bombs make us realise that we are all fellow travellers, that we all need each other, that we can rely on each other, then something very good will come out of all this."*

All quotes from *Out of the Tunnel*
by Rachel North (Friday Books, 2007)

None of us can know for sure that there won't be another attack. The chance of being on a targeted train is tiny, but it exists. Nothing we can do can ever guarantee us total safety. So there is a rational basis for our fear, and it cannot be wished away.

Naturally, we each make our own decisions about the risks we are prepared to take, but knowing our fears are not completely irrational may help us to feel less ashamed of our anxieties, a bit less critical of our reluctance. Less shame and less self-criticism may enable us to feel a slight sense of hope, enough optimism to join those having a go, sufficient willingness to take that first step.

If you want to be able to travel by tube, then there are several things to take into account to make it easier to start.

| There are times when the underground is much busier than usual. Although station staff and traffic police are brought in to assist at the worst times, for example when football crowds are expected, unless you really want to go 'cold turkey', and plunge right back into the fray, you may want to start outside peak travelling hours (peak times are between 7-10am and 4-7pm in Central London, as a rough guide). Late night shopping evenings are also likely to be crowded, especially before Christmas. According to London Underground, the peak use of the system is the first full week of December, with shoppers adding to the number of commuters still working.

However, it's probably not a good idea to go when there is absolutely no-one else around, or to try travelling in a completely empty carriage. Find a time that works for you.

2   You may wish to break 'taking the tube for the first time' down into microsteps, for example: visiting the booking hall, buying a ticket to go up and down the escalators, watching the trains go by from the platform, noticing the time the doors take to open and close, and so on. If this is what will help you most, London Underground advises that is 'very sensible' to tell station staff what is intended - to avoid 'looking suspicious' to fellow passengers, to staff or on CCTV cameras …

3   Choose your station and your route. Check the *Transport for London* website and use the Journey Planner before you travel, to see that the line you want to take is running smoothly (www.tfl.gov.uk). You can ask London Underground Customer Services (see resources) to send you a free copy of the incredibly helpful '*Getting Around London: Your Guide to Accessibility*" which will show you which stations have street access, stairs, escalators, and lifts (or found at http@www.tfl.gov.uk/assests/downloads/getting_around_london.pdf). If you have difficulty getting on or off

the train, the website also suggests that you travel in the first carriage, so that the driver can see you and allow you more time.

4   It's worth remembering that only forty-five percent of the tube system is underground; you may be able to get back on the tube by getting used to the other fifty-five percent first! - at least then you know you can 'use the Underground'. Some lines are very close to the surface (known as 'sub-surface') even when they go underground along some of the line, for example parts of the District, Metropolitan and Circle Lines. So train carriages are larger than on lines which are totally or largely underground. These trains go in and out of tunnels, so you can check with London Underground how many of the stations are actually underground, or how many tunnels there are on the journey you want to make.

5   Take a buddy with you. Discuss beforehand what you would like to do, and how you would like them to support you. Remember this is your agenda, your experiment, and you can choose at every step of the way whether to proceed or not. You might surprise yourself by being able to do more or go further that you'd thought, so plan in that possibility, as well as an early end to the trial if necessary.

6   Despite the unspoken *'no talking on the tube'* rule (see above), give yourself permission to talk to other people if you start feeling panicky, to ask for help. Check out who is around anyway - who might be good to ask? Who looks approachable? Who looks friendly? Who might *you* be drawn to help, if things got tough? Noticing who is around you can help to 'ground' you in the actual experience of where you are, the reality of 'now'. London Underground

runs a poster campaign offering support from staff if you feel unwell, so feel free to approach them for assistance.

7 Standing near the door with an opening window can at least give you best access to whatever air is passing through the train. It's also possible to see out, and to develop knowledge of your surroundings if you are at the stage of wanting to really ground yourself in the reality of your experience (*there's an advertisement for moisturiser, there are the wires on the tunnel wall, there are fingerprints on the window, the train is going quite smoothly and I'm fine, I'm breathing in and out, I'm fine ... and so on*)

8 London Underground advises passengers to carry water, and you might also consider carrying a small pocket torch. In Japan it's common practice to carry a small battery operated fan. Some companies even sell small 'commuter kits' for underground travellers, including items such as drinking water, a flashlight, a whistle, an anti-dust particle mask, and wipes for face and hands (visit www.survival.box.co.uk). If you take something to read, choose material where people cope with difficult situations, not simply get overwhelmed (see p. 151). Carrying cards with affirming messages can be helpful, or notes from people who love you, to read or simply to envisage sitting in your bag or pocket (see Resources) or make your own portable 'calm pack' (see p. 149).

9 London Underground is aware of the importance of keeping the public informed about what's going on, and that there will be people on board with a diversity of needs and concerns. So train operators are trained to make announcements within a short time of the train coming to an unscheduled stop, and then regular announcements as necessary.

It's good to know this natural need for customers to be reassured by the human voice is taken seriously. For people who experience claustrophobia, knowing that there are chains of connection going on outside the confined space, with people taking care all along the system, with someone DOING something about the situation, this is a great relief. We can follow these people with our imaginations as they do whatever they do to get things moving again. Reminding ourselves of the operator's expertise and training: his or her connection to control staff: *their* connection to all the other services which support and protect the system, and their collective intent to make travelling by underground as safe and efficient as possible, helps to humanise the experience, enabling us to feel less isolated.

10   Finally, if you want a lateral way to start getting used to the idea of taking the tube, try visiting the award winning www.london-underground.blogspot.com, created by 'Annie Mole'. This is full of the most interesting, useful, fascinating, irreverent, useless, funny, moving and surreal information, opinions, and facts (and songs) about life on the London Underground (and the worst excuses for delays, 'etiquette' for tube travel) you could ever imagine finding - and more. Designed to remind you that you are absolutely not alone - as soon as you enter that station, you are part of a vast travelling community.

As we move forward in overcoming claustrophobia, we sometimes make plans, take things cautiously step-by-step, get it right and get it wrong, and sometimes things just happen. The first time I tried to go back on the Underground, all geared up with bags full of emergency supplies, heart full of screwed-up courage and mind full of racing thoughts - the train didn't go in a tunnel where

I thought it would. I had travelled the overground section of the Hammersmith and City line, anticipating entering the tunnel just before Paddington. We left Royal Oak. Terror started in my belly, my visualisations deserted me, I started sweating profusely, thinking I'd scream - and then - and then, nothing. No tunnel. The train glided serenely on and pulled up at Paddington. In broad daylight. I stumbled off the train and collapsed in a heap on the platform. *No tunnel.* No sense of mission accomplished. Damn. *Damn.* All that adrenaline and will-power for nothing. And far too agitated and fearful now to feel like trying again.

But of course it wasn't *'for nothing'* - I could learn a lot, even from this apparent 'failure'. The fact was that I had envisaged going into a tunnel for the first time, and *stayed on the train* with the intention of going through, things I hadn't done in years. I could also recognise how far I'd departed from the *actual* experience of what was happening, by bracing against the *anticipation* of the tunnel. We hadn't even been in one! - my imagination had created the whole experience. Noting this helped me further differentiate between fear created by reality, and fear stimulated by my mind.

Signalling to my unconscious my *willingness to have a go* has been an enormous step forward in itself, and even if there was no actual tunnel, to have acted on that willingness was tangible evidence of progress. Once I'd realised all this I went to Yo Sushi! at Paddington to celebrate (psyches thrive on rewards of many kinds).

The next time I went back on the Underground was not with the first person I might have thought of as a buddy, but rather an old friend who happened to be there on the day I decided I'd have a go. I'd been walking and breathing and singing and chanting and reading emboldening books (*see* p. 115) and I knew that today was it. I knew that I was further ahead with my willingness to take the next step, and that *that* was a step in itself, so I'd already made yet more progress. I couldn't really lose. We came out of our meeting, had a cup of coffee, and I 'warned' her that I had given myself permission to turn back at any point. She said fine, was very matter of fact and moved the conversation on to other things.

I would have been pleased if I had managed to get as far as the (underground) Euston ticket barrier. To my amazement, despite the profoundly strange sensation of having legs made of jelly, and completely oblivious to all the direction signs, we went down the escalators, onto the train, stood by the door with the window open, watched the doors close, sped through the tunnel, travelled six stops (including *under the river*) and then were out again in the fresh air of an overground platform.

The first time through tube tunnels in seven years. Completely ordinary, and for me, utterly extraordinary. We stood on Vauxhall station, and I stared at my friend as if she were an angel. I was in shock, a shock of delight and amazement, pride and gratitude, and we hugged and we whooped as if we'd just won Olympic gold.

Subsequently I've been back on the tube with other friends, other journeys. Practising noticing which line and which platform rather than being guided through almost in a trance: sitting rather than standing, sitting in the middle, rather than at the edge, travelling in different compartments, keeping all my clothes on (as opposed to ripping everything off down to a level of minimum decency): and finally, eventually, travelling alone. Feelings come and go - sometimes almost easy, other times much, much harder.

Sometimes I simply don't fancy it. I may even choose avoidance as my tactic du jour. What's interesting is doing this no longer affects my ability or willingness to go back to the underground, at other times. Recently I've even drifted off to sleep on the underground, unthinkable in the only very recent past. For some people it's either/or - total avoidance or total re-immersion.

Some theories would suggest this is necessary. But for others of us, it's a more random path, and that's fine. What works for you? Each experiment is a triumph, more learning, more tangible experience, more notice taken of *what's actually going on*, rather than what our imaginations create as fantasies of *what might be going to happen*.

I don't always like it. But I can do it. And that's the liberation I hope for you.

Finally, the most encouraging words that I have found about travelling by underground are from Rachel North, whose writing after the London Underground bombs has encouraged so many people, including me:

> *"Today, lots of people on the Tube will be worrying about what if and whether they'd cope, and I'll know I did cope, we all coped, which is kind of empowering really. We just tried to stay cool and trust we'd be safe soon."*
> From *Out of the Tunnel*
> by Rachel North (Friday Books, 2007)

FLYING

Within our anxiety, about what may happen to us if we become trapped in a small or confined space, there is often a kernel of truth. In the case of flying, it's true there would be little any passenger could do if there was an incident or accident, beyond co-operating with the crew and fellow passengers, and 'remaining calm'. So, we won't fly and keep ourselves grounded, if we read *potential of danger* as *inevitability of danger*. But if you want to travel, for holidays or business or to see your son in Sri Lanka, you may also need to set alongside one set of facts *another* set that shows that flying is one of the safest means of transport there is.

Here are ways contributors who've experienced claustrophobia manage plane journeys:

"Get a seat on a plane with plenty of leg-room"

"I try to avert my attention when the doors lock just before take-off"

"Focusing on the 'end product' - the likelihood of an enjoyable holiday. I also chat to the stewards if I'm feeling nervous before take-off (I mostly actually enjoy taking off!)"

"My main method is familiarisation and knowing some facts and trying to rationalise - for example, that noise is the under-carriage going up, statistically flying is safer than driving, why would anyone choose to be a pilot or hostess if they expected to die in the job; that hostess is clearly not terrified (or even anxious!). It's FFR - factorise, familiarise, rationalise" (see p. 120)

"I've come to quite like that time-out-of-time cocoon feeling you get on planes. It's similar to when you're in bed and not too well but not too ill either, a kind of warm, suspended animation".

"I concentrate on the regular hum of the engine and not on the erratic bumps of the turbulence. I suppose it's like self-hypnosis"

"I picture the sea-gulls over the estuary near my home, and imagine the plane from a distance in the same way"

"I try to imagine I'm on a coach rather than a plane!"

"I always tell the cabin crew if I'm going to the loo, as I don't want to open the door and find the exit blocked by a trolley".

It helps to learn about basic principles of flight and to remember what incredibly sophisticated feats of engineering planes are, built by professionals dedicated to safety. Planes don't stay airborne through luck or wishful thinking! (though pilots and cabin crew may be unaware of the number of passengers working hard to keep their planes in the air through the power of positive visualisation). It helps to remember that the pilot is highly trained, that he probably enjoys his or her life and would like to live it for a long time. It helps to remember that he or she probably doesn't consider flying to be an extreme sport. It may help to envisage the pilot, once you've heard his or her voice, and to imagine the calmness and efficiency with which he or she is doing the job. And to picture the ground crew and air traffic control staff at each airport monitoring and controlling and communicating with each plane - once again, we are part of a community of travellers, and not alone.

Looking at the attendants and noticing how relaxed they seem to be can be reassuring. Although not always. One dark and drizzly night coming home from Marseille, I asked a rather miserable-looking hostess what the weather was like back in London. *"Terrible"* she sighed. *"Gusty and stormy. Probably be a very bumpy flight"*. !!!!!! Presumably missed the training modules on *Calming* and *Soothing*.

Nonetheless, the vast majority are helpful and informative, and trained to help passengers with diverse needs, including claustrophobia. There are many helpful books on overcoming fear of flying, and uniquely amongst modes of transport, courses (*see* Resources).

EUROSTAR AND EUROTUNNEL

Eurostar was cited by many contributors to this book as the means of transport they would most like to be able to use, but daren't. It's understandable. Long tunnels underground, under the river, the estuary, the sea ... perhaps it's comforting to know that the expert tunnelers hold a special ceremony when they build each new section of the tunnel, displaying a refreshing humility toward what they are about to do:

> *"It's a recognition that a tunnel is a majestic piece of infrastructure and it has high risks attached to it, and therefore it's important to recognise it and honour it".*
> Mike Glover of Rail Link Engineering,
> quoted in The Observer, London, 30.09.07

If you choose to use Eurostar, there are many strategies in this book for dealing with the journey. It may also help to know that according to Jon Williams, of Eurotunnel Passenger Customer Relations, issues of claustrophobia were taken into account when the shuttles were designed, and that every effort was made to make carriages as light, spacious and airy as possible. He goes on to say:

"We do, however, appreciate that everyone's experience of claustrophobia is different, and whilst some customers who are generally affected can travel with Eurotunnel with no ill-effect, others may not be as fortunate.

If a member of the train crew is called, they will, of course, be sympathetic, and having assisted customers with similar experiences before, will offer as much information, assistance and advice as possible. We can confirm that we usually have at least one first-aid trained member of staff on each shuttle, and anxiety attacks and hyperventilation are covered in their training.

While not all of the staff on board will have had this training, a very large majority of our train crew have been in their positions for quite some time and even those without specific training will have experience of advising customers who may be affected by claustrophobia"
(Email communications,
20th February & 6th March 2006)

Perhaps it would be the cherry on top of the icing for you to travel to Europe through the tunnel - perhaps because that's where I had my major scare all those years ago, it has been mine. I wish you very well in your journey.

Chapter 10

Finding support through therapy

*"I so much wanted to be cured that I was not ashamed to ask
    for help"*

*"I've never thought of seeking help. It just seemed like a
    practical personal problem I had to work around, like a
    physical impairment"*

*"I didn't want to see a therapist. I wanted to keep the problem
    invalidated - seeing a therapist would have made it too
    real, too much of a thing"*

The attitude of people who experience claustrophobia towards therapy
varies, from positive acceptance to outright rejection. The National
Phobics Society* (survey Autumn edition 2007) found that many
people with phobias did not use therapy because of lack of knowledge
about different approaches. Others felt too ashamed to ask for help,
or found the cost of private therapy prohibitive. Some contributors
to this book have tried different forms of therapy, to greater or
lesser effect. No one therapy comes out as the best for everyone.

*"My GP, a consultant, a CPN and my counsellor were all
    excellent"*

* *see* Resources

"A therapist came from America and asked for volunteers.   He made me go in a lift every day about twenty times and then said I was cured.   When he went back to America I was as bad as ever."

"I was told that the anxiety level would drop after a certain time, but it didn't".

"I'm currently seeing a therapist who specialises in Cognitive Behavioural Therapy.   My therapist showed me that it is not possible to cure claustrophobia quickly.   It is a slow deliberate process to unlearn the negative thoughts that have built up over the years.   As I have worked through my problems with my therapist it has become clear that the fear is out of all proportion to reality."

"I was happy with both the 'therapies' (I've experienced). *They both helped in a number of ways.   It was good to have my fear acknowledged and taken seriously.   I didn't mind about asking for help, in fact I was glad there was help available."*

"I saw a therapist as a matter of necessity - I had to be able to fly - we were being transferred abroad for my husband's work."

"I saw a therapist for about six months and she helped a lot.   It took much longer than I'd initially thought, but I was paying, so fortunately I had a choice of how long I could go for."

"I mentioned claustrophobia in my therapy, but I didn't go there specifically for that, I went for other things. It helped to the extent that the therapist took it seriously, and because the overall therapy enabled me to take up all kinds of life-challenges, claustrophobia has been just one of many things I'm tackling."

"I haven't (asked for help) so far, because I would prefer to avoid the situations that cause me anxiety. However, I've recently found out about the possibility of CBT phone sessions through the National Phobics Society"

If you do want to try therapy, having some knowledge about the different ways of working may enable you to choose an approach that appeals to you, if you have a choice. There is absolutely no shame in accessing support. Accepting help to move beyond the life-limiting effects of claustrophobia is an act of courage. After all, if we can publicly name our realistic fears and reduce our phobic anxiety, we will be in a better position to help others.

So you can go to your GP for referral for therapy for claustrophobia. If you do, the kind of therapy you will be offered is likely to be limited to one or two alternatives, and there may be a waiting list for assessment and treatment (waiting times vary from one month to a massive eighteen months, according to where you live). You can also become a member of the National Phobics Society, which has a register of therapists experienced in working with phobia. Waiting times are very short (approximately two weeks) and there is a sliding scale for fees. Or you can find a private therapist.

If you decide to take up therapy on a completely private basis, you have the right to know about your therapist's qualifications, and whether he or she is registered with a professional association, which will have training standards for their members, and a Code of Ethics. If you are not happy with the therapy, or the therapist, you can leave: no one approach is right for everyone, and if the therapy is not helping, it may not be the one for you. In the unlikely event that you need to make a complaint, the professional association will have a formal procedure.

It's important to remember that regrettably! therapy is not magic, nor the therapist a magician. *No single therapy has been found to work for everyone.* The more likely indicators of a successful outcome of therapy are your own motivation, how much you trust the therapist, how much support you have outside the therapy sessions and what else is going on in your life. So the more you can work on any aspects of these, the more likely you will be to find therapy helpful.

The work you'll do in therapy may not always be comfortable, and results may not come as quickly as you'd like. What you should be able to feel, however, is that the therapist is a professional person, on your side: someone you can trust, who sees your claustrophobia as the problem, and not you. It's probably not helpful to see a therapist who insists they can 'cure' your fear (fear is a natural, essential human response to threat, and we do away with it at our peril). Or one who insists that your claustrophobic response to confined space, their dangers and discomforts, is entirely irrational (however slim the chance, accidents and incidents can, and regrettably, do happen).

Our work in therapy or through self-help is to be able to stop avoiding and to deal with our fears as they occur, not to convince ourselves that life is totally safe or that we will always be totally fear-free. Once de-mystified, the best therapeutic ideas are the application of common sense, with support. So as well as attending formal therapy sessions, there is a huge range of practical strategies you can try out by yourself, or with a supporter, many of which are included in Chapter 8. So by the time your name comes up on that NHS waiting list, you may not need the therapy!

Here's a guide to the key therapeutic approaches tried by people who experience claustrophobia.

COGNITIVE BEHAVIOURAL THERAPY

"My CBT therapist was patient and thoughtful and prepared to devote time in the most practical way, for example by accompanying me on several journeys on the Underground, in hospital lifts and even to wait sympathetically whilst I struggled with the terror of locking myself into sealed-cabin loos."

"The method was to ask the patient to make a list of twenty or so frightening situations in order of horror, you were then asked to tackle the least formidable of these and if successful, to proceed to the next up and so on. The weakness of this scheme became apparent when we could not get, say, from situation 15 to situation 14. I learned to lock myself into our own car, but to relax in the rear of a childproofed car? No way."

If you seek medical support because you experience claustrophobia, out of all the so-called 'talking therapies' in the UK, you are most likely to be referred for Cognitive Behaviour Therapy, or CBT. The National Institute for Clinical Excellence (NICE) (the body that provides guidance on promoting good health and preventing and treating ill health), recommends CBT as the treatment for phobia in general. This doesn't necessarily make it the best approach for everyone, but it is considered cost-effective and is one of the best researched 'treatments' for phobias. You are likely to be offered up to seven sessions, with some services extending this. Alternatively, you may be offered computer-assisted CBT (CCBT) which is an internet based interactive system called *FearFighter*, designed to help you to help yourself through CBT (for more information on *FearFighter* and the pros and cons of Computer-assisted therapy, *see* p. 219). Because CBT is the current treatment of choice in the NHS, I have covered it in most detail, and also looked at some of the reasons why it may not be effective for everyone.

As the name suggests, Cognitive Behaviour Therapy will help you identify how your thinking affects your behaviour, and your feelings. Your therapist will work with you to find more constructive ways of viewing the situations you fear. You will be encouraged to carry out experiments to test out your thoughts, or theories, on the assumption that you'll find evidence that contradicts thoughts of doom and terror. You will be supported to gradually build confidence in your ability both to tolerate fear and make more accurate assessments of the kinds of situations you want to be able to face. You will be encouraged to re-visit the situations you fear in a systematic way. You may be taught relaxation or mindfulness techniques, and you may receive some 'psycho-education'; learning simple information about what happens to your body and mind when your feel anxiety can help you recognise how your 'symptoms' and reactions are quite normal and natural.

CBT regards changing the way we think as the key to changing how we feel and what we do. The CBT view of phobia is that our belief, that we cannot survive the terrors we experience in small spaces, is faulty. CBT suggests that the belief that we won't survive is held in place through the behavioural strategy of avoidance, which also serves to maintain our scared feelings. If we allow ourselves to stop avoiding, to go back into a small space, we might find our theories are wrong, and *our fear of our fear* unnecessary. We might find that we don't feel as much fear as we thought we would, or that we are still able to think and function even when we are feeling frightened.

So a Cognitive Behavioural Therapist will help you to think about your thoughts, and the feelings that the thoughts stimulate. He or she will help you understand how some thoughts provoke uncomfortable or distressing feelings, and how other thoughts can maintain that negative state.

Different kinds of thoughts that may be challenged include

1 Selective abstraction - where we only choose to pay attention to aspects of our environment or a situation which confirm our belief that catastrophe will or is about to happen (*"The lift doors are creaking, they're not closing as quickly as usual, the light is flickering, therefore I'm going to get stuck"*)

2 All-or-nothing thinking (*"If I go in any lift I'll get stuck, if I avoid lifts I'll be safe"*)

3 Over-generalising (*"I got stuck in the one lift so I'll get stuck in all lifts"*)

4 Magnification (*"It will feel absolutely terrible if I get stuck"*)

5 Discounting (*"Even though I went in the lift last week with Sarah it was only for a minute, it doesn't count"*)

6 Personalisation (*"The lift I take will inevitably be the one with the bomb in it"*)

7 Imperatives (*"I should be a stronger person who never feels fear"*)

Clients may be encouraged to keep a thoughts and feelings diary, to uncover what kind of thinking is helping to maintain anxiety. This will provide material to learn how to challenge distorted thinking both within the therapy sessions and outside, whilst doing homework. A thought diary helps the client to notice the *effects* of thinking a particular kind of thought on her feelings and choice of behaviour - to see what kind of thinking supports, motivates and encourages her, and which deflates, defeats and restricts.

With the therapist, you will be able to uncover your beliefs and create real-world experiments to test them. This will mean re-experiencing and being exposed to fear. You can do this all at once, in a method called 'flooding' (*see* p. 226) or alternately, you can break the challenge down into small steps, small increasingly difficult stages (looking at a picture of a tube train, going to a tube station, going to the platform, entering the train and leaving again, going one stop with a therapist in the same carriage, going one stop with the therapist in a different carriage and so on) until you can manage your goal, in the process of systematic desensitization (*see below*).

One absolutely marvellous aspect of CBT is that it is one of the very few therapies in which the therapist may well accompany you out into the real world, to help you try out the claustrophobic situation you've been avoiding! - a real and tangible support for many people. Of course you'd need to know that you can also go back to those situations with someone who isn't a professional, and then try it on your own, to see further progress, but this first supported attempt can break the ice of years. In this way, CBT can be a very normalising, matter-of-fact way of working, which may suit many people.

Safety behaviours

A *safety behaviour* is defined as a way in which we protect ourselves from experiencing anxiety in the problem situation. Some therapists believe that anything we do to minimise our anxiety is counter-productive, and likely to perpetuate our phobia (our anxiety about confined spaces).

What might a safety behaviour be, for people who experience claustrophobia? It could include any or all of the following:

1   Avoidance
2   Distracting yourself from whatever is making you anxious
3   Performing relaxation exercises, or doing controlled
      breathing
4   Reading confidence-building affirmations from cards when
      you feel anxious
5   Self-soothing, with thoughts, words or touch

*Each and every one of these strateg*ies has been found useful by people who have experienced claustrophobia, and have been recommended by experienced practitioners, including CBT therapists. However, some CBT practitioners hold the belief that safety behaviours like these need to go, if you are to truly overcome your phobia. Some will recognise that it is difficult for many people to go 'cold turkey', that is, to give up all their safety behaviours at once, and may suggest a gradual 'withdrawal', although purists suggest that this could be deepening the problem.

You may be presented with this approach, so it's worth understanding it a little better.

One way to think about the concept of 'safety behaviours' is to think about how people use a 'St. Christopher'. A St. Christopher is a little locket bearing an image of the patron saint of travellers. If people who believe in this tradition carry or wear the locket, they feel safe to travel. If they lose it, they might feel afraid to travel, believing that it was the locket that really kept them safe, and not their own abilities and the absence of mishap.

So I might, for example, use the 'safety behaviours' of carrying a book each time I fly, to distract me from my worries about the doors closing, or practising relaxation techniques if I felt my anxiety beginning to rise. The *'no safety behaviour'* theory suggests that I would believe it was the reading and relaxation that had previously kept me safe and that I might suddenly re-experience the fear of being trapped, and be no better off, or even worse than before.

So the aim of eliminating safety behaviours is to enable someone to experience the full force of the anxiety the safety behaviour was meant to keep at bay. Practitioners using this method believe that it is only by feeling this, and discovering that we neither die, have a heart attack, go mad, fall apart, or make fools of ourselves (or anything else we fear will happen) that we will overcome the fear of our fear.

In *Manage Your Mind,* (Oxford University Press, 1995) Butler & Hope advocate getting rid of safety behaviours as part of their four-step strategy for overcoming phobias. Their four steps are:

1 Work out what you are doing to protect yourself (safety behaviour)

2 Make a prediction - "if I didn't protect myself by (doing one of the safety behaviours) - what would happen?"

3 Carry out an experiment - decide how the prediction could be tested, and then do it

4 Think carefully about what happened - analyse the outcome of the experiment and what has been learnt about the prediction. Base the next experiment on the result

Butler & Hope suggest that you will feel anxiety during this process, but can do it in stages, and that thorough preparation at Steps One and Two will enable you to find that changing (your behaviour) *"can be more like exploring a new way of approaching the world than entering the lion's den"*. This is encouraging stuff. They give us the example of Ellie, who is fearful of small spaces, including: the shower if she is alone in the house, theatre, cinema, planes and rooms without windows, or where other people block an easy exit. Ellie *'knows perfectly well'* when she's out of a claustrophobic situation that her fears will not *'drive her to breaking point'*, but began to doubt this when in a small or confined place.

> *"So she knew she would have to make herself feel the fear in order to test the prediction. She decided to shut herself in the cupboard under the stairs and to stay there for two minutes when her husband was at home. He agreed to be the time-keeper."*   (ibid, p.224)

Ellie stays in the cupboard for the whole two minutes, after which her husband opens the door. She has felt terrified, with all the classic symptoms of high anxiety, but she has noted all her symptoms and looked out for any indication that she was losing control. Despite all these unpleasant feelings, Ellie ...*"did not call out, or scream, or lose control in any way."* Clearly Ellie has learnt a lot from this experiment, and goes on to be able to use a shower, stay in her kitchen when there are several people with her, and plan further experiments in order to use the tube-train.

There are several things we can note from this experiment which may be helpful for those of us who feel anxious at the very thought of going in a cupboard. My sense is that Ellie is obviously at the point where she can maintain her 'internal witness' whilst feeling anxious. This, along with her ability not to 'call out or scream', would suggest that her phobia is relatively mild, or that she has already done a lot of work prior to going in under the stairs. Many of the people I have talked to in my research would have been 'calling out' *"NO!"* long before they had even got their shoulders in the cupboard!

1   *Ellie decided on her own experiment.*   As I've been emphasising throughout this book, we need to find our own way to deal with claustrophobia, choose our own experiments. Approaching challenges as experiments can engage our curiosity.   With no pre-defined outcome, we are in the business of learning about ourselves, rather than defining how we should behave or react.

2   In choosing the cupboard-under-the-stairs, Ellie was being *inventive and lateral,* using resources close to hand, practising domestically before moving on to more unfamiliar ground. We can practise the skills we need to deal with small and confined situations in all kinds of ways (*see* p. 134).

3   *Ellie time-limited her experiment.* Unless you're going for the full flooding approach, this is often sensible. As adults, reminding ourselves how long something will last, and that '*this too will pass*', is a great strategy.

4   *Ellie had her husband alongside for support.* There are numerous people who will help us in our journey away from claustrophobia - we don't have to do it all alone. Our memories of their presence and the help they give us may be sustaining when we try other experiments without support (*see* Support networks p. 148).

5   *Ellie is encouraged to talk about her experiences afterwards.* Talking about what we've done not only enables us to make the most of whatever learning we can gain from the experiment, but it's also a great way of discharging some of the built-up tension and adrenaline and of gaining support and affirmation. Hearing yourself describe what you felt and experienced can be a good way of defusing residual anxiety, and later, your listener may be able to remind you of your earlier success, if you're feeling discouraged. We're natural story-tellers, and describing what happened gives us the possibility of experimenting with different ways of telling the tale. We can make it into an epic action movie, a comedy routine, or a simple tale of quiet satisfaction in taking one more courageous step. We can feature how hard it was, or we can highlight our resourcefulness and what we did that helped us cope. When the story is 'out there', we can reflect on it alone or with someone else, and work out what to do next. It can help us reach out to others, either for further help or by sharing our experiences, offering encouragement to others.

Rachel North, for example, was on the Piccadilly line train targeted by a suicide bomber in London on 7th July 2005. She wrote an online blog about her experiences that inspired and encouraged many people in the days and weeks that followed. Subsequently, having found writing an incredibly helpful means of making meaning from her experiences and reaching out to other people, she wrote a book - *Out of the Tunnel,* (Friday Books, 2007), which I highly recommend (and *see* returning to the Underground p. 184).

6   *Ellie's way of coping in the cupboard was to pay "close attention to her symptoms, watching for signs that she was losing control"* What Ellie has taken on here is a role and a task. Her role is to be an experimenter, testing out a theory. In extremely frightening situations of genuine danger, professionals such as firemen, policemen and ambulance drivers say that they were able to carry out their duties because they have a role to perform, one that they had practised for over and over again. Whatever they might have felt, and however much they might have wanted to run away, they 'had a job to do' (*and see* p. 170 *for more on roles*).

Ellie's task is to notice what happens to her - she has a variety of classic anxiety symptoms, and she also notices that once the cupboard doors open, these symptoms decline rapidly. Having a task in a situation of high anxiety and panic has frequently been observed to be very useful. It has long been military strategy to keep soldiers busy with drills, taking their equipment apart, cleaning it and putting it back together again, or even digging holes and filling them in, before they are sent into battle.

So two strategies can be learnt from this that anyone can try.

(i)   The first is to sign yourself up as an experimenter, whose job it is to find out what works for you in your aim of overcoming claustrophobia. You can play with what kind of experimenter you want to be - a full-time one, a part-time one, one who works in a team, has an assistant or who works alone. One who records everything there is to do, or one who keeps a 'diary of success' (see p. 123). One who rewards himself when an experiment is conducted, one who takes care of herself by taking exercise and having fun in between experiments, one who does it all wearing a red nose. Your job, your way of doing it.

(ii)   Within this overall role, there will be many tasks - and one
        of these can be noticing. Noticing is something you can
        practise at any time, not only when you are feeling anxious.
        Noticing what is happening in your body. Noticing what
        thoughts are travelling through your mind. Noticing what
        is going on in your environment. Noticing what makes you
        anxious, and what makes you laugh. Noticing what you
        enjoy and what gives you pleasure. Noticing whether the
        glass is half-full or half-empty, or whether you're fed up
        with glasses and want a beer-mug!
        Notice that noticing doesn't mean adding in imaginings
        (although you can notice and enjoy your imagination as
        well). Noticing your heart rate increasing doesn't mean
        leaping to conclusions that you are just about to have a
        heart attack and that therefore you must get out of the
        situation at all costs to save your life. Noticing is factual
        and emotionally neutral (*"that's interesting, my heart is going
        faster"*). On the other hand, it may lead to practical action
        - *"I notice that the wheels on the coach in which I am travelling
        back to the airport (at 3.00am in the middle of Turkey), are
        on fire - so I'll get off "* for example - one of my all-time
        favourite decisions.

So each time we do anything towards helping ourselves overcome
our phobia - *"I wonder how I would feel if I look at some pictures
of caves? I wonder what it would be like to sit one seat in from the
aisle at the cinema? I wonder whether I would feel better asking
Mike or Mel to come with me to the dentist?"* - we're gathering
information about what works for us. The more we know about
ourselves, the more we know about what works for us, the more we
can know how to take care of ourselves, even in small and enclosed
spaces, even if we become trapped.

It could be said that having a role and having a task were, in fact, safety behaviours, like any other. So to me, the proof is in the pudding, in real world action. If you manage to get on the train you've avoided for years because you took a book, a bottle of water and a watch with big luminous hands, (or even a friend with big warm hands) and you distracted yourself with the book, sipped the water and occasionally looked at your watch, or chatted to your friend, the end result is that you have travelled on that train. You've done it once. You can rightly feel an enormous sense of pride and satisfaction. That is a real world experience, an indestructible memory to draw on next time you try to take the train.

Yes, you used three or four safety behaviours! and you may wish to experiment another time not taking a book. Or it might be that if you forgot your book, as I might have done in the example above, you might look for something else to read, knowing that reading helps you. Or if there was nothing to read, you might think about books you've seen reviewed or something you read last year (*and see* p. 152 *for more on books*). Or you might talk to the person next to you, or hum a tune, or watch the grass move beside the tracks.

The point is that it was your inventiveness that enabled you to make the journey, you've made a memory you can draw on with pride. Whether you accept the '*no safety behaviour*' approach or not, you may wish to experiment with this perspective. Exercising choices, trusting our intuition whilst also taking on board other perspectives can all enable us to reinforce our view of ourselves as resourceful, solution-finding people.

Is CBT good for everyone?

Despite all the excellent techniques CBT offers, not everyone finds it useful. This could be for a number of reasons. Firstly, it tends to offer a largely 'one-size-fits-all' specific number of sessions, which may not be sufficient for some people. This may be especially true if the person has experienced a complex trauma, or if he or she has a history or personality that might make accessing support, trusting the therapist or being organised enough to do homework, difficult or impossible.

Secondly, its reputation as the NICE recommended therapy can get in its own way. If clients feel it is not working for them, they may secretly blame themselves, or feel the more despairing *"especially since my phobia took on CBT and came out on top"*, as one contributor puts it. Therapists who buy into *the 'only one evidence-based approach that works'* school of thought may equally see any problems which arise in the course of therapy as being about the client, rather than the method being inappropriate for this individual, or something about the relationship between therapist and client being amiss.

The therapy may require the patient to 'score' their improvement week by week. As one contributor put it,

> *"It is human nature to wish to oblige those who are trying to help you or at least to seem politely grateful, which I was. But I was not being truthful when I acceded to this ratchetting up of the score each week".*

If the patient does not feel their anxiety is diminishing, but wants to please, they may complete the therapy without letting the therapist know that improvement was at best, superficial. CBT does not as yet pay much attention to the relationship between therapist and client, as a process through which the client's difficulties can be understood, as other therapies do, and may miss this dynamic.

CBT practitioners are often not required to have therapy themselves, and this will become yet more true if CBT is offered by social workers or nurses. Therapists from disciplines that do insist on this requirement know that it is one of the most valuable aspects of their training. Being in therapy yourself is probably the only real way to fully understand the therapist-client relationship from the client's perspective. It can give the trainee therapist a taste of how difficult it can be not only to *make* but to *sustain* real change, to battle with genuine fear and terror, and how frustratingly and mystifyingly slow progress can be. It can show the trainee therapist that what they might think of as the client *'resisting treatment'* or *'not making use of the therapy'* is just as much affected by who the therapist is and how he or she behaves towards the client, as it is by the client's nature or personality.

Thirdly, not all trauma is accessible to conscious thought, so body-based therapies such as EMDR and other non-verbal techniques may give greater access to deeper layers of the problem than the cognitive, especially if dissociation has taken place (in the 'freeze' mode).

Fourthly, as described above, some CBT practitioners will encourage the experience of 'staying with' feelings of anxiety, on the basis that if you stay with them long enough (between thirty minutes and an hour), they will recede. From a neuroscientific perspective, however, many non-CBT practitioners would state that we are not 'designed' to remain in states of high anxiety, bathed in what William Bloom vividly describes as the 'acid bath of chemicals' (in *Feeling Safe,* Piatkus, *2002*) - we are designed to use them up in effective action. 'Staying with' stressful feelings of anxiety can, in some cases, impair the immune system, and create stress for the heart. For people who have experienced deep trauma, PTSD or have early experiences of abuse, neglect, trauma and insecure attachment (*see* p. 58), this may be inappropriate; they may require a longer and deeper therapeutic relationship than CBT alone can offer. Equally, staying with stressful feelings can create secondary traumatisation for the practitioner; personal therapy or supervision would help the practitioner notice and care for themselves in this situation.

CBT depends on the patient's ability to continue to hold onto thinking in anxiety-producing situations, and to think between sessions and after the series of sessions has finished. If you are able to think while you are panicking, even if is simply to remind yourself to stay in the situation or to notice what you are feeling, then you are already well on the way towards overcoming your claustrophobia. It is perhaps these people for whom CBT is most effective.

However, this may be very difficult for people with poor self-esteem or high self-doubt. Additionally, those who have experienced early trauma, neglect or loss experience great difficulty in accessing the frontal lobe region of their brains, where calm, logical thinking takes place: in situations of high stress or anxiety this difficulty is heightened. If therapists are not trained to observe the body of their client, nor their own bodies, vital cues may be missed (although this may be changing with interest in mindfulness and body scanning techniques, already practised within some other therapies).

Finally, claustrophobia, as with other forms of anxiety, may be a symptom of wider or deeper unconscious difficulties or conflicts. CBT will focus on the presenting problem - that is, if you're referred for symptoms of claustrophobia, that will be the focus of treatment. Such focus is welcome, but treating the symptoms alone may not reach far enough. Conscious thought processes may not be the whole story, and improvement undermined if the therapist is reluctant to consider 'the bigger picture' when 'treating' the presenting symptom. Such dynamics may make the work more complex than the usual seven sessions allow.

Despite these caveats, CBT is a robust, well-researched and incredibly helpful therapy. It may be effective as a stand-alone practice, or in more complex cases, as one tool integrated into a wide repertoire of others by experienced practitioners from a variety of therapeutic backgrounds.

CBT is available within the NHS, privately and at low cost to members of the National Phobics Society either face-to-face or on the telephone.

COMPUTER-AIDED THERAPY PROGRAMMES AND RESOURCES

There are increasing numbers of programmes appearing on the internet and as stand-alone CDs designed to help people with anxiety and phobias. An advantage of using a computer is that there is an interactive element; the programme can be personalised to your particular thoughts and experiences, and your own input can be incorporated into decisions about the next step to take.

As new self-help information becomes available, it can be quickly incorporated into the programmes, which are often highly visual and even fun. Computer-aided therapy is anonymous, private, and can often be accessed from home at any time. It cuts down patient travel time, and may be of assistance to those who don't want to seek medical help, or feel that to do so would be stigmatising (*"I didn't see a therapist, I just used a machine"*). Computers don't have to look riveted by their clients' problems all the time, and are likely to be infinitely patient (although they can freeze and crash). And of course it is likely to be highly suitable for people who like computers!*

---

* An excellent book on this subject is *Hands On Help*, by Marks, Cavanagh & Gega, (Psychology Press 2007)

The downsides are the mirror image of the benefits. If you don't like computers, or if you're visually impaired, this isn't likely to be for you. Computers can't notice subtle cues, nor offer the kind of healing that some people will only find through a supportive, empathic relationship with another person. Some people drawn to computers also have a tendency to avoid human contact, which may be the very issue underlying or maintaining their claustrophobia. In many programmes, you'll be required to do between four to five hours homework, so people who have problems with self-starting, motivation or organisational skills may have difficulties. Computers can't switch issues, nor pick up profound underlying difficulties; you must stay focused on this one problem, regardless of what your actual needs are at the time. Finally, there is the ever present issue of computer security. Whilst every effort is made to guarantee anonymity, no system is perfect.

From an NHS perspective, computer-aided therapy reduces the need for face-to-face contact with professionals, so there will be cost savings: you would, however, be offered contact with a clinician at the outset for assessment. Some systems are also arranged to offer telephone or email contact.

Computers also offer the possibility of chat rooms, online discussion groups, email support, computer-aided vicarious exposure, and virtual reality experiences. So this relatively new form of therapy will undoubtedly continue to expand and develop, fantastically broadening the range of our options.

The programmes described below are just two of the many now coming online. Each will have benefits and drawbacks, and different aspects of each will appeal to different natures and personalities, but may be worth exploring if computer-aided therapy appeals to you. Of course it will still be up to you to follow through with real-world action, away from the computer!

FearFighter (FF) is a computer-aided therapy programme which guides the user through nine self-exposure steps over ten sessions, and is available through the National Health Service. It is recommended by NICE (National Institute for Clinical Excellence) for managing phobia. It is designed to be accessed over the internet, at a surgery or at home. After assessment by a health practitioner, you would be given a password to log onto a personalised programme (introductory information is available on the site without requiring this). You can use *FearFighter* over about ten weeks, as often as you like or at least once a week. You may or may not be offered additional face-to-face contact with a therapist whilst going through the programme.

In *Fearfighter,* the rationale for exposure therapy is explained, and you are supported to identify what your particular issues and goals are. There are homework diaries, feedback on progress and 'trouble-shooting advice'. Little or no experience with computers is required.

FearFighter encourages the user to follow these five principles:

1   Decide what triggers your fear
2   Personalise the trigger
3   Set goals to face the triggers and the fear they produce
4   Do each goal long enough for the fear to diminish
5   Do each goal daily if possible until it's less frightening.

The programme consistently encourages the user to stay with fear, not to run from it, as a way of breaking an 'addiction' to escaping and avoiding panic. It assures people that the panic is likely to peak and then reduce over thirty minutes or '*at longest, an hour'*.   An example is given of a 'first goal' for people who experience claustrophobia, getting used to being in lifts. *Fearfighter* suggests the following goal: *"Stand in a lift with the doors open by yourself for forty-five minutes four times a week"* http://www.fearfighter.com/fearfighter%20light/2-12.htm

Personally, I suggest that you check with the building's security staff before you adopt this strategy! *FearFighter* does acknowledge that for many people who experience claustrophobia, the first goal is more likely to be simply looking at the outside of a lift. So as ever, it's important to find your pace, your way forward. This programme has been extensively researched and has the same efficacy as existing face-to-face services, so it is seen as cost-effective.   For more information, speak to your GP (*and see* Resources).

Waysforward is a Solution Focused self-help computer-based programme (*see* Resources, *and for more on* Solution Focused Therapy, *see belo*w). The programme asks a series of questions, helping you reflect on and identify what you are already doing to overcome your phobia. It enables you to think about what might constitute the next step, what might help you take it, and visualise what life will be like when you've done so. The programme collates, summarises and provides a print-out of the answers you've given. Although this is simply your own words presented back to you, the responses you've given have been arranged in a simple, uncluttered way, with answers from different questions logically juxtaposed into what amounts to a self-made prescription for future action and success.

If we feel anxiety rising when we're faced with yet another confined space, it can be difficult to hang onto or even remember the fact that we've already made huge strides in dealing with our phobia. This programme can usefully support the development of our 'internal witness', reminding us of past experiences of success, and noting what works for us now. Jonathan Hales, the Solution Focused therapist who designed *Waysforward*, says that people who use the programme often comment *"I didn't know I was doing so much"*, a realisation that can only serve to raise self-esteem and confidence. In other words, the questions can lead to a sense of satisfaction that you've already thought of helpful things to manage your phobia, reinforcing hope that you have the problem-solving skills to continue to make improvements. (For example, *"How did you manage to do this?, "What else do you do?"*, and *"What difference does it make when you do this?"*)

This approach mirrors therapeutic solution-focused thinking, which enable people to recognise their own strengths and creativity, rather than looking to 'outside experts' to solve problems for us in a 'top down' way. Hales puts it this way: *"It's great for rebels: for people who want to work things out for themselves, who hate being given advice"*.

Other sites worth visiting
www.moodgym.anu.edu.au
www.livelifetothefull.com

EMOTIONAL FREEDOM TECHNIQUES
The Emotional Freedom Techniques concept was developed in the US in the 1990's by Gary Craig, and arose out of Thought Field Therapy (TFT, see below). EFT (Emotional Freedom Techniques) is a relatively new member of what are sometimes described as the 'energy therapies', and can be experienced with a trained practitioner or be practised - for free! - on oneself (*see* Resources). Like TFT, its focus is on restoring natural balance to our minds

and bodies, releasing feelings that may continue to distress us. For people who experience claustrophobia, this would be the sense of anxiety we associate with confined spaces. Practitioners suggest that EFT clears 'stuck' energy from our bodies, by acceptance and release, and that it is unnecessary to know how the process works to benefit from it.

The therapist will ask you to think about the issue you are bringing, and to notice how you feel. You will then be shown which acupressure points on your body to tap lightly. Some practitioners may tap their own bodies at the same time, to keep in tune with you. You are also given some words to say, relating to your issue, which are thought to assist the process of dispersing the stuck emotion. You would then be asked to think about the upsetting situation again. There may be a reduction in the intensity of feeling you had when you first thought about the issue.

The process can be repeated on that occasion or over different sessions to further reduce the reaction. The process may uncover other feelings, and these can be worked through as they emerge. Language is important in EFT: skilful therapists will use key phrases and relevant words for different aspects of the problem. You won't have forgotten about whatever situation caused your distress, but you may no longer feel the same anxiety when you think about it, freeing you to go back to similar situations afresh.

In the hands of practitioners who recognise the importance of the therapeutic relationship, this new technique promises to be of great interest and value. You may still wish to pace your return to confined spaces, after this brief intervention, to give yourself time to know that the treatment has been effective.

EFT is now available in the UK, within some sections of the NHS, privately, and through the National Phobics Society.

EXPOSURE/SYSTEMATIC DESENSITIZATION

The aim of this form of therapy is to 'acclimatise' to the fear we have been avoiding, by going back to the situations we fear in a systematic way. (*Fearfighter* is an example of a computer-aided form of this kind of process, *see* p. 221). In some forms of this therapy, patients are first taught relaxation skills to control fear symptoms as they arise, and in CBT (*see above*), cognitive strategies for coping with distorted thinking. The patient and the therapist establish a 'fear hierarchy', with the least frightening aspect of the problem as the first task to be faced, and the most difficult at the 'top' (and *see* p. 27, and Appendix A). He or she is then encouraged to practice using the relaxation skills and cognitive strategies to enable him or her to face each situation or anxiety trigger in turn, first of all in the imagination, or through pictures, and then by re-visiting each step in reality until the fear response has died away. This can be repeated before attempting the next step.

Other uses of this process include inviting the patient to imagine the worst thing that could happen when faced with the next trigger, and then to contrast such 'catastrophizing' with what actually happens. The ability to realistically assess situations and to more accurately predict outcomes can develop in this way.

The huge advantage of this form of therapy is that the therapist may be willing to escort you back in to the situations you fear, giving you tangible experience of success. This form of therapy will not focus on any issues that might be underlying or lateral to your claustrophobia. The length of therapy will vary, according to the depth of your fear, although if you are referred to this form of therapy within the NHS, the number of sessions you are offered will be limited. It is likely to work best where people have good external support systems, are motivated to work in a focused, goal-oriented way, and where there are not underlying relational issues, or complex post-traumatic stress disorder.

Flooding is an extreme form of exposure therapy: two contributors express these views

"I don't believe facing your fears head on can possibly work, otherwise we'd all be better straightaway. I had no choice but to stay through my terror, and lived to experience the terror receding on the other side. But it worsened rather than relieved my feelings."

"It does work within a limited period - for example, on a long-haul flight you have to deal with it. The faithful valium plays a part but habituation does too because I don't pop pills all the way there. But every journey sees a new beginning - the acceptance learned earlier is not transferred forward."

In this technique, the individual voluntarily enters the situation viewed as most frightening, with a therapist, and stays in the situation until the sensations of terror peak and then subside, as they are assured that they inevitably will. The individual thus has information that terror can be survived. The idea is that once you have this information, you will no longer feel so afraid of your fear. Equally, you might be asked to describe a trauma you have experienced, in great detail, and to repeat this until you no longer experience any associated negative emotions.

Some people may find this strategy effective. In their most feared situation, they face their worst anxiety - that their fear will be intolerable, that they will die, disintegrate or go mad, or do the wrong thing: but they survive. They don't die, and they don't go to pieces. Armed with this knowledge, they no longer feel they have to avoid the fear-provoking situation.

This is the full Monty version of *'getting back in the saddle'* after a fall. Many commuters did precisely that the morning after the London bombings in 2005, as a proud act of defiance of terrorism, and solidarity with the people killed and injured in the blast. There are many web blogs describing their experiences, including from those who were actually in the trains where bombs were planted, but who, knowing they had survived, decided to use their anger and pride to overcome the scare of travelling again. However, it may be that having the role of *'defiant Londoner'*, *the* solidarity of fellow passengers and the task of *'not letting the terrorists win'* were supportive in this instance (see *tasks* and *roles* above, and on p. 170). In full-on exposure therapy, 'safety behaviours' are not recommended (see p. 208).

Many of us have a different experience - that the 'full flood' of anxiety does not follow the patterns suggested, or that even if it does temporarily 'peak' and diminish at the time, that the anxiety can subsequently return just as powerfully. The knowledge that we have survived once does not seem to 'stick' or diminish our anxiety about feeling fear again. There are many trauma specialists who would suggest that use of this very direct technique, if mishandled, could run the risk of the person dissociating or becoming re-traumatised, possibly at a deeper level (*and see* Appendix B). This makes sense, if we think about soldiers and emergency service staff suffering post-traumatic stress disorder. If 'flooding' worked for everyone, then the 'cure' would be to simply send them back to war or into another emergency. Equally, the therapist may run the risk of experiencing secondary traumatisation, being exposed to someone else's sky-high anxiety without reprieve. Imagining it is desirable or possible to completely distance oneself from this effect is unlikely to be helpful to either the practitioner or the patients.

However, if you want to try this technique, please seriously consider taking broad professional advice before doing so, especially if your phobia is long-standing, or was caused by trauma of some kind.

EMDR (Eye Movement Desensitization Reprocessing)

This form of psychotherapy was developed by Francine Shapiro twenty years ago, and has established an excellent track-record of success, often in a short space of time. It uses a structured eight-phase approach to deal with powerful memories of the traumatic experience that continue to cause distress, nightmares, flashbacks and the natural desire to avoid similar circumstances that can lead to phobia.

Practitioners believe that such traumas have not been fully processed or integrated into our ordinary conscious memory, but were so overwhelming that they had to be 'held' in a separate 'place' in our memory systems. They are readily re-activated by triggers resembling or associated to the original incident. Shapiro points out that when people have nightmares of such past trauma, they are not only being re-traumatised by their own unconscious, but they are also losing precious sleep*. Sleep is one of the main ways in which we process and make sense of our experience, especially the phase when we experience rapid-eye movements (REM sleep). If we are deprived of this kind of sleep, we become more stressed, more prone to tiredness and agitation, and more vulnerable to anxiety.

EMDR therapy offers a way of addressing emotions, thoughts, physical sensations, attitudes and behaviours associated with the memory. It provides a way of 're-processing' them more effectively,

* in EMDR, 1997, Basic Books

so that we are then able to face what has happened, and the future, with more equanimity. We may still have feelings about what happened, but we will not experience them in such a debilitating way. Our systems relax, and we can move on, developing key skills and new behaviours and attitudes for the future. In the case of claustrophobia, we might then feel able to contemplate the return to confined spaces, and do so unburdened by our past experience.

EMDR is an 'integrative therapy', using a skilful combination of aspects of cognitive, behavioural, psychodynamic and interactional therapies. In addition, as the name suggests, it uses side-to-side eye-movement, although as the therapy has developed, bi-lateral sound or touch has been included as well, so the name is a little misleading. Theories about why this therapy works suggest that this technique, within the supportive context of the therapy, may be enabling the two halves of the brain, the more logical and the more emotional, to re-engage in the normal process of integrating experience. The therapy is non-intrusive, and emphatically does not require the client to describe the trauma in detail, to 'stay with' hugely painful feelings of distress for lengthy periods, or do homework. Enabling the client to take care of themselves through relaxation, and building a relationship of trust and safety between therapist and clients will take priority over 'processing' in the early stages. The importance of the relationship between the therapist and client is stressed at all times.

The EMDR process will address past, present and future aspects of the issue. The process ends when the client has a real sense that there is resolution; positive thoughts need to be 'believed' at a deep body level, just as the negative associations to the trauma were. The speed of the process is directed by the client who can stop at any time. EMDR has shown consistent and long lasting improvement with many people who have experienced post-traumatic stress disorder in recent conflict, accident and emergency situations, as well as those whose experiences of trauma are from long ago in the past.

One of the great benefits of EMDR is that whilst speed is not the primary goal, it will become quickly obvious whether the process is helping you or not, so if you decide to find a private therapist the cost may not be prohibitive. EMDR can also work with issues underlying or maintaining claustrophobia, if these emerge as memories of the first trauma are 'processed'. EMDR is available in the UK, within some sections of the NHS, privately, and through the National Phobics Society (*see* Resources).

HYPNOTHERAPY

"I tried hypnotherapy and did a Fear of Flying Course. Both helped although the hypnotherapy was relatively short-lived in its effect. But I still use one of the techniques, of thinking of a particularly good time."

"The hypnotherapist has been an enormous help, helping me to relax and to understand that I wasn't always claustrophobic - it was learnt and can be unlearnt"

"I have given hypnotherapy several attempts (two practitioners both employing the same imagine-you-are-flying-above-the-rooftops-and-descend-into-a-beautiful-garden scenario, half a dozen visits each). There was no measurable improvement. I have also been encouraged to talk about past crises and what might have set them off, but with no practical advice."

"Having had hypnotherapy, I am, if not cured, much better. In the last three weeks I have been in tubes and lifts with only a little discomfort."

"I tried a hypnotherapy tape and the speaker said I wouldn't be able to move my leg, but I could, which didn't inspire confidence! However, I listened to the tape a few times, and although I often fell asleep, I started to find travelling by train quite a lot easier, so I think it helped."

The aim of hypnotherapy is to allow the patient to enter an altered state of consciousness, reached through a process of deep relaxation. The state is not dissimilar to the feeling of being deeply immersed in music, or a pleasant day-dream; some experience this as a sensation of floating, others as a warm heaviness. It is generally experienced as pleasurable. The hypnotic state or trance is facilitated by the therapist inviting the patient to follow a systematic whole body relaxation, and/or to concentrate on the patient's breathing, the therapist's voice, an agreed image, or a combination of these.

This won't happen until you and the therapist have had time to talk through your difficulties and what you are hoping for from the therapy. So there's no need to feel you will somehow lose control as soon as you see the therapist. Some clients also use hypnotherapy to prepare themselves to go through a situation they anticipate may be difficult for them, for example having an MRI scan or going on a long journey by plane.

In this hypnotic state or trance, normal judgement and defences of cynicism and suspicion are suspended. The patient's sub-conscious mind may be accessible to positive suggestion intended to mobilise and activate his or her inner resources (to deal with the problem issue). Practitioners will never make suggestions that would be detrimental to the health and well-being of the patient. It may also be possible to re-visit traumatic incidents without the patient being exposed to the powerful negative effect of associated feelings, and without the need to talk about what happened. The sub-conscious can be provided with alternative, helpful imagery - for example, images of a place that the patient knows well and considers safe; consequently reducing the effects of the trauma in conscious awareness. In this way subsequent experience of confined space becomes less likely to 'trigger' anxiety.

The depth of trance and the effectiveness of the hypnotherapy will depend on the skill of the therapist, and the quality of the relationship between client and therapist, which needs to be one of trust and rapport.

Hypnotherapy offers the possibility of deep relaxation, both at the time of the therapy session and as a portable technique to be accessed before entering or whilst in a confined space. Visualisation has been found by many to be a helpful technique (*and see* p. 171). The client can be guided through an imagined 'rehearsal' of each situation she wants to go through, seeing herself do so successfully, and equally importantly, experiencing what it's like for it to be over. Hypnotherapists may also suggest the client 'anchors' a positive feeling state, for example by squeezing a finger, and breathing evenly.

In some areas, Clinical hypnotherapy is available on the NHS. The National Phobics Society (*see* Resources) offers low-cost hypnotherapy to members. To find a private hypnotherapist, contact the National Register of Hypnotherapists and Psychotherapists.

MEDICATION/DRUGS/RESCUE REMEDY

Medication is rarely used for long term treatment of phobias, although some drugs are given for long-standing and pervasive anxiety. If you go to your GP for assistance with claustrophobia, you may be given medication with a tranquillising effect to help you cope with a specific situation, for example, a long international flight. Some of the contributors to this book have taken this route on occasion. You would not be given this kind of drug for lengthy periods, because this can lead to dependence. 'Self-medication' with alcohol or 'recreational' drugs is not advisable, in that your ability to handle an emergency, should it arise, could be compromised. Some people have found that taking 'Rescue Remedy' has been helpful, homeopathic drops with relaxing properties, available over the counter at pharmacies. It is advisable to seek medical advice before taking any new product.

PSYCHODYNAMIC THERAPY

The term psychodynamic suggest movement between different elements of our psychological selves, between our internal and external worlds, our conscious and unconscious minds, between what happened to us in the past and what may be happening in the present.

Psychodynamic therapists will work with claustrophobia that has arisen from 'straightforward' trauma by providing an attentive relationship in which you can explore your thoughts, feelings, and experiences. You will be supported to make your own decisions about what you want to do to overcome the phobia.

However, psychodynamic therapists may also view claustrophobic feelings, at least in part, as an expression or projection of what might be 'going on' in our internal worlds. Our fear of confined space may be part of a much wider picture, the symptom of a distress that is too difficult to express in any other form.

For example, we may have had a distressing experience in the past that we have never been able to speak about to anyone, and felt very alone, unsupported, overwhelmed, and/or ashamed. What happened, and the feelings we were left with, 'get in the way' when we try to deal with situations in the present that somehow remind us of that event. If what happened involved being confined, physically or emotionally, we may transfer those past feelings onto actual present day confined spaces, or a small incident that happened there. We may have no more trust that we will be helped in the present than we were in the past. Our fear responses become amplified, a mixture of past and present, and we become phobic.

Alternatively, we may feel trapped in our present life-styles, jobs or relationships, but have neither the skills to free ourselves up, the belief that we have the right to do so, or the confidence that we could cope with that freedom. Our claustrophobia may be more about feeling that parts of our personality or aspects of our emotional range are trapped, unable to come out into the full light of day, than about actual physical confinement.

"Throughout my life I've dreamed that I was trapped - usually buried alive. I wake in total panic and often find myself trying to open a window or if I'm in a strange room, in a hotel or a friend's house, I'm scrabbling at the wall where there should be a window. I don't know where any of it comes from, but I'd like to"

Psychodynamic work will help us become aware of blocks in our patterns of behaviour, thinking and feeling responses, and in how we handle relationships. Once these blocks become conscious, they can be discussed and explored within the safety of the therapeutic relationship, enabling us to express feelings and resolve painful conflicts that have been buried or suppressed. We can reflect on their meaning from a new perspective. We can grieve for what cannot be changed, find new attitudes to what has happened and to the people involved in what happened. We can be supported to experiment with new ways of bringing about constructive change in our day-to-day lives.

Psychodynamic therapists may invite you to work with memories from the past, your dreams, your associations, your thoughts, sensations in your body, with projective techniques such as art or writing, and much besides. The therapist can support a client who has never felt that they have had a reliable, empathic person they could really trust, to find out what happens when such a person is willing to be available and present with them. This can be difficult. Trust can take a long time to build where it has been shattered or never firmly established in the first instance. We may need to repeatedly test the relationship, to find out if the therapist really can accept all the different sides that make us who we are. A moving depiction of this process is given in the film *Good Will Hunting*, in which Matt Damon plays the client to Robin Williams' therapist (although not all therapists would use precisely the same techniques as the Williams character).

If claustrophobic feelings are a representation of another, deeper conflict, then once the core of the conflict has been uncovered and worked through, the claustrophobic feelings should fade away. Psychodynamic therapy ends when the client feels ready to let go of the supportive relationship with the therapist, and is able to derive more fulfilment and satisfaction in real life.

Some psychodynamic therapists will present themselves as

the 'blank screen' of the analytic stereotype, but most experienced therapists work with a wide array of strategies and are likely to be more human and less mechanistic. Therapists use their own responses to understand what is happening inside you and within the therapeutic relationship between you, and may well share their reflections with you.

There can be a public perception that this kind of therapy reduces every experience to the lowest common denominator - usually sex or death, to paraphrase Woody Allen. This is the actual experience of one of the contributors to this book:

"The doctor referred me to a counsellor who tried to say I had a deep-rooted sexual problem and came to the same conclusion every week (I didn't, that was what was annoying)"

No experienced therapist would ever impose 'interpretations' in this way - let alone such a cavalier pseudo-Freudianism (Freud himself believed that phobias were caused by an accumulation of sexual tension, produced by abstinence or by frustrated sexual desire, and that the phobia was both an expression of the anxiety and a defence against it*) .

Clumsy interpretations aside, some people find it helpful to work with the idea of projection, from inner world to outer experience. After all, by allowing our claustrophobia to restrict where we go and what we do, we are acting in a self-limiting way. By avoiding, we effectively make our worlds smaller. By resisting the possibility of feeling fear, we are shrinking the range of human emotions we are willing to experience. We can never

---

* see *Fear: A Cultural History*, by Joanna Bourke, Virago, 2005

be precise when we try to do that - restricting our openness to one feeling can have a knock-on effect on others. Our avoidance may be part of a wider pattern of how we relate to life in general, and to other people. We may feel we have been abandoned, in early or recent relationships, or we may secretly feel that we have abandoned part of ourselves. We may have all kinds of unexpressed feeling and conflicts, and be carrying an enormous burden of stress and pressure around with us. When we're faced with a confined space, we may be afraid those feelings will have nowhere else to go. Here are some thoughts from contributors who found there was more to their claustrophobia than confined spaces:

"I think I have always had a claustrophobic personality. I used to feel hemmed in by certain situations - family holidays and other gatherings from which there was no escape."

"When I explored my situation in therapy I realised that my difficulties probably went back to when my parents died within two years of each other. Each time (there was a bereavement) *I was pregnant and I now feel I did not grieve fully for* (my parents)*"*.

So here are some questions to muse upon, either alone or with someone to support your enquiry into claustrophobia. Whatever insights you come up with can be explored in thought, in conversation, or through painting, drawing, collage or drama, whatever works for you. They may point you in the direction of what you want to do next.

How do you feel about being alone, separate from others?

About being with other people? Do you trust others to help you when necessary, to keep you in mind when you're apart? Do you have to behave a certain way to keep people close? Have you lost someone precious to you?

What messages did you receive as you were growing up about being safe, resourceful and effective in the world? Did you get enough? Do you need more? What messages did you receive about your ability to problem-solve?

Do you keep yourself confined to a small world, a limited number of people you know and places you go, a small range of activities and interests? Or do you allow yourself to be curious, to take risks, to explore and experiment, to have huge pleasure and excitement in your life?

Do you feel trapped in some part of your life, or do you 'trap yourself' in anyway? Are you dealing with that situation, or are you somehow avoiding it? Do you need some support?

Psychodynamic therapy can also help us to address the thorny question of whether we may be *gaining anything* by being claustrophobic. So if, for example, our claustrophobic feelings may lead us to persuade our family to only behave in certain ways (for example, prioritising our need to sit in the front seat, always take stairs, never fly and so on) then our role in the family shifts somewhat in the direction of becoming the-family-member-with-the-greatest-needs. We find ourselves exerting a degree of control over other people's behaviour. We're getting support and to some extent, becoming the centre of attention.

If we overcome our claustrophobia, we will lose that role and give up that form of control. If that leaves us feeling anxious, or diminished in some way, it may be that the claustrophobia was, at least in part, a displacement of our more general need to be recognised as a person with a separate identity and authority. We may not have the skills to communicate our need for support directly, or feel we have a right to the kind of attention we need.

All this can be hard to think about. People may feel either indignant or ashamed. It needs to be stressed that claustrophobic feelings are frequently 'straightforward' responses to the effects of trauma, and won't be expressing 'disguised' needs. However, this kind of therapy can help if we think there may be something going on below the surface, and want to have a look, enabling us to reduce the risk of self-sabotage. We can learn to express our full range of needs directly, and will have a better chance of both resolving our claustrophobia, and having other needs met more satisfactorily.

Psychodynamic therapy is likely to last longer than say, CBT, EMDR or Hypnotherapy, and thus be more expensive. The length of time needed could be frustrating if you 'simply' want to address your claustrophobia. It is highly unlikely that the therapist would offer direct strategies for dealing with claustrophobia or that they would accompany you to try out experiments. You will need to re-visit confined spaces yourself. However you may feel more confident to do so as a result of the therapy, or to ask for support, if this was once difficult. Psychodynamic therapists are required to have their own therapy, so are likely to have a deep understanding of the challenges of being 'a client'.

Gestalt, Integrative, Cognitive Analytic, Creative Arts and Attachment-oriented therapists and counsellors are all likely to use psychodynamic thinking as part of their practice, although naturally it will be strongly influenced by the theoretical model in which the practitioner has trained. For more information about each kind of therapy, or to find a therapist or counsellor, please visit the websites of the United Kingdom Council of Psychotherapists (UKCP), or the British Association for Counselling and Psychotherapy (BACP), telephone or write to them for more details (*see* Resources).

RE-BIRTHING VIA 'CONSCIOUS BREATHING'

Re-birthing practitioners* believe that for some individuals, claustrophobia can be traced back to a birth trauma. The client is encouraged to breath in a style known as 'conscious' or 'connected' breathing, with the therapist alongside, and to allow his or her body to experience and release tensions as they arise. These tensions may arise from past trauma. Some clients going through this process notice a powerful feeling of constriction, crushing, and even pain, which practitioners link to experiences in the womb pre-birth, as well as during an actual delivery. The therapy process can take up to two hours, and may be repeated four or five times over a few weeks until a deep sense of relaxation is achieved.

With the release of tension arising through this process may come an awareness of deep-seated body-based associations (confined space = danger) formed at the time of the birth trauma, before thinking. If we recognise that these associations result from historical trauma, we may be able to re-assess their validity in our current life and release them. This may enable us to change our attitudes, and mean less tension and anxiety about encountering future small spaces.

The disadvantages of this kind of therapy are not only that it can be hard to locate an experienced practitioner (as opposed to someone who has 'done a birthing weekend'), that it is expensive

*see Resources

and not at all likely to be offered on the NHS!! - but also that it's central theory - that we can connect with birth trauma by breathing, and go on to fundamentally release that trauma - has not been proven. Other trauma that happened after birth may be stored in the body, and it may only be our belief that it is actually a 'birth trauma' we are re-experiencing. Also, releasing physical tension may not lead to the relief of trauma, or to a deep re-assessment of our beliefs that small spaces are threatening. We would still need to start to re-visit such spaces and test ourselves out before we could really know if the therapy had had positive effects.

Whilst such a therapy might not be available or appropriate for everyone, practitioner Bronwen Astor encourages anyone to find out what your birth was like. If you learn that there was indeed a problem with your delivery, you might find this knowledge a relief. Something did happen, and your anxieties could possible have been formed at a time when you were extremely vulnerable, in the face of genuine threat. You might be able to see connections between what actually happened to you, and what you believe today about confined spaces, or indeed about other life situations (for example, facing a confrontational situation in which you feel there is little room for manoeuvre). Says Bronwen Astor:

"*You may also be able to remind yourself that you're not that vulnerable anymore, and that you have all kinds of adult faculties and skills that could help you if you were ever to be trapped again. You've experienced the worst, and you made it. You can make it again*".

Whether metaphor or reality, images from birth trauma revisited could give you another route for self-awareness and developing constructive self-support.

SOLUTION FOCUSED THERAPY

This form of therapy values the client as expert, not the therapist, and supports our ability to sort out our own issues with our own abilities, resources and motivation. No history taking is necessary. At the first session, practitioners will ask for a simple description of the issue and what changes the client has already made in the direction of solving the problem prior to the meeting. Practitioners focus on using precisely the client's own language, and on facilitating the client to find solutions in the direction of the stated goal. Clients will be encouraged to do more of what is working already, and to identify exceptions to the problem - (*"Is there any time that was a little less bad than all the others?"*) from which to draw suggestions for potential solutions.

Clients will be asked what they think, not what they feel. What's known as problem-talk (that is, dwelling on the difficulty) will be gently interrupted, or the client guided to focus on what strategies they used to cope. The implication of the therapist's attitude is that change is inevitable, and that the client has the ability to find solutions. The therapist may pose questions that directly imply that the problem is resolvable - *"What will you be doing when the problem is solved?"* The presence of solutions is to be favoured, not the absence of problems.

The problem will be scaled numerically (*"Where are you now, if x is worst and y is best?"*) and clients asked to identify how they will know when they have moved up a point in the direction of positive change. They will also be asked what difference significant people in the client's life will notice about the client's changed behaviour or mood. The therapist may ask the 'magic question', to encourage creative thinking: *"If you woke up tomorrow, and everything was perfect, what would be the first small signs that the problem has changed? How would you notice things had changed?"* - or ask the client to look back on their current problem from the position of themselves as a wise old person who gives good advice to their younger self.

Solution focused work is likely to be brief, and sessions may be at irregular intervals in order for you to put any new solutions into practice. This kind of therapy is supportive of your strengths, highly focused on helping you reach the goals you identify.

Some Solution Focused practitioners work within the NHS, and private therapists can be located via professional organisations (see Resources, *and see WaysForward*, p. 222).

THOUGHT FIELD THERAPY

Thought Field Therapy (TFT) is a relatively new form of therapy that claims to be able to offer rapid and dramatic improvement with phobias, sometimes in as little as one session. A 'thought field' is described as the body-brain-feeling state we experience when we have a particular thought. It is generated by our body's nervous, hormonal and chemical responses and the cognitive activity related to the thought. If we think about a negative experience, unpleasant physical, mental and emotional responses are generated across the thought field. So, for example, if we think about a time when we got trapped in a crowded airport corridor or in a queue for passport control, we may re-experience a sense of the negative and unpleasant feelings we had at the time - sweating, racing thoughts, churning stomach and so on. The fixed trauma is thought to create ripples of negativity, and to block the body-mind's natural tendency to heal itself.

TFT practitioners suggest that instead of suppressing these negative reactions, distracting the person from them or teaching coping techniques to deal with them, Thought Field Therapy can eliminate these negative ripples completely, aiming to render the memory of the experience neutral. If the Thought Field is 'cleared', the person won't be so anxious about approaching other similar situations, such as going through an airport, as in the example above. The treatment consists of the application of a unique 'code', a sequence of thoughts, eye movement and body tapping, individually created for each patient through a diagnostic procedure. Tapping focuses on the energetic meridians of the body, as EFT does (above), but here the sequence and order of tapping is much more important, and language less so. The procedure is painless, and said to work even if the patient doesn't 'believe' in it. Some practitioners are developing voice-based treatments, said to be as effective. Paying attention to body and mind is likely to be much more powerful than verbal means alone.

At present TFT is usually expensive for private treatment: on the other hand, if, as practitioners suggest, only one or a short number of sessions are required, it may be cost effective in the long run. You may still wish to pace your return to confined spaces, after this brief intervention, to give yourself time to know that the treatment has been effective.

TFT is available through the National Phobics Society, and has recently (2007) been accepted as eligible for inclusion in the NHS Directory of Complementary and Alternative Practitioners. The British Thought Field Therapy Association (BTFTA) is the recognised organisation for qualified practitioners (*see* Resources).

Chapter 11

Beyond claustrophobia

Claustrophobia is a challenge. It can take time, effort, energy and courage to find our way out, but we can find inspiration from others en route, however different their circumstances. On being liberated earlier this year, Alan Johnston, the BBC journalist, said that whilst he was imprisoned, he had been encouraged by messages from other former hostages, Terry Waite and Brian Keenan. His own comment is similarly supportive:

> *"Both of them were an inspiration, [with the idea] that you will find reserves inside you that you didn't know you had. We all have it and you do find it."*
> www.jerusalemites.org/news

Very few of us will ever have to find the depth of reserves these three men required, to deal with fear in confined spaces, but in our own circumstances, we can find the internal and external resources we need as we gradually make progress in dealing with claustrophobia. The rewards of doing so are enormous:

✔ An increased sense of expansiveness, excitement and hope
✔ Freedom to decide where we want to go and what we want to do, unconstrained by anxiety about what we might encounter
✔ A greater sense of relaxation and peace of mind

✔ More self-knowledge and self-trust
✔ Greater clarity of thought, calmer feelings and increased
   confidence in our powers of both assessment and self-care
✔ The opportunity to contribute to supporting others, and to
   improving our environment

All these gifts are waiting patiently for us outside the limits claustrophobia imposes.

Finding out what works for us doesn't have to be grim, formal or technical, and we can gather ideas from many disparate sources to inform our choice. Not having choices was one of the aspects of being confined we feared. When we can choose - how to respond, what to think, what to do, who and how we love - we can recognise choice as one of the most important aspects of freedom, and appreciate expressing it. In suggesting how Alan Johnston might cope with being free, Brian Keenan put it beautifully - "*Choice is, after all, the crown of life*" (The Guardian, July 9th 2007). We can take our time: what we choose and what we do matters.

Learning from the contributors to this book was a huge help for me, and I hope that you too will have found support in knowing that others are walking similar paths.

"*Experiencing claustrophobia was awful and overcoming it very difficult, but in the end it was well worth it*"

"*It is possible to overcome claustrophobia. I have been so bad I could not travel in my own car with the door closed to now being able to fly alone. I have never not gone into a claustrophobic situation but have needed an alcoholic drink and have fought to control my feelings*".

"I went to the Edinburgh Tattoo. Nine thousand people trying to get out and it didn't worry me at all"

"The therapy and support has enabled me to be free of claustrophobia for a long time"

"I strongly advise fellow sufferers to try the therapies on offer. Subscribing to the National Phobics Society is great, as you feel less isolated and you are given access to the various therapies. It makes you realise that it is possible to overcome your fears and improve your quality of life"

"Advice? - don't deny it. Discuss your feelings with others who are sympathetic and/or share your anxieties. That way, any 'stigma' will fade as one realises one is not alone and in some ways our feelings may be perceived as quite logical or 'normal'"

"Sharing experiences in groups helps people to realise they are not alone with their experience"

"Don't give into it, use positive self-talk and all the anti-panic techniques you know"

"I remember when I got into a glass lift with my therapist for the first time I was terrified at the thought of doing it. However, the experience turned out to be not unpleasant. It's all about being brave enough to take the first step. This has shown me that however hard it seems or however depressed you get, there is always

hope. You just need some guidance and encouragement. And if I can do it, then anyone can"

....

I wish you very well for your own journey out of claustrophobia. And who knows, when you make your first trip on Eurostar, I might be that woman across the carriage from you. So please smile - it will help us both.

APPENDIX A

CREATING A HIERARCHY OF GOALS

Step 1

Look at the list on pgs. 22-25.

Which situations can you already deal with well?
    Tick as many as you find

Which situations would you like to be able to deal with better?
    Circle between five and ten.

Which situations do you think you'll never want to deal with?
    Strike them through

Step 2

Transfer the items you've circled on pgs. 22-25 to Grid A on p. 251, writing the easiest (or least difficult) situation at the bottom, working your way up in degrees of difficulty to the hardest item at the top. (Of course you can always add other situations, if they don't appear on pgs. 22-25).

Step 3

Each goal can be broken down into micro-steps, little experiments with confined space. Visualise yourself going to first situation on your list, and notice at what point your anxiety is triggered. Becoming able to deal with that anxiety is your *third* micro-step.

Please write it in Box 3 in Grid B (examples of micro-steps are given on p. 176 and 189, for going into lifts and using the underground).

WHAT SUPPORT MIGHT HELP YOU TO TAKE ON MICRO-STEPS 3?

Learning more about the actual risks or mechanics of the situation?

Asking a friend or professional to go with you?

Identifying a reward to focus on?

Doing some relaxation exercise beforehand?

Moving into 'researcher' mode, to find out whether your prediction, of how hard taking the step will be, is true or false?

(Check the self-help section on planning (p. 124) for suggestions). Write your preferred options in the box alongside Micro-step 3.

You might choose at this point to start experimenting with micro-step 3, in reality, or fill in the boxes for micro-steps 4 onwards, or you might want to practice self-soothing and slow breathing to calm the anxiety you may have just felt by thinking about your goal. You can include as many micro-steps as you require, on the way to achieving your goal.

SO WHAT ABOUT MICRO-STEPS 1 AND 2?

Even being *willing* to think about a situation that has made you anxious can be a huge step. It represents a shift in your psyche, a tiny re-orientation deep in your unconscious, in the direction of expansiveness and hope.

So that was micro-step one, and you can fill it in Box 1, and give yourself a big tick.

Actually *thinking about* the situation, visualising it in detail, was micro-step 2.

Again, another big tick, alongside Box 2. Two successes already. You're on your way.

GRID A   Hierarchy of goals

10	
9	
8	
7	
6	
5	
4	
3	
2	
1	

GRID B   Micro-steps and support   ✔

STEP 1		
STEP 2		
STEP 3		
STEP 4		
STEP 5		
STEP 6		
STEP 7		
STEP ... as many as you want		

APPENDIX B

POST-TRAUMATIC STRESS DISORDER

Post-traumatic stress disorder (PTSD) is the name given to a range of symptoms a person experiences after a traumatic event, which persist for a protracted period. In some cases, symptoms do not emerge until some time after the event. The disorder may continue until the person receives appropriate medical or therapeutic support.

Complex PTSD usually describes the effects experienced when the person was unable to escape a traumatising situation, and may include ongoing situations of abuse, neglect or bullying that persistently erode the individual's normal coping mechanisms as well as when one-off, single traumatic incidents have compounded pre-existing difficulties.

Symptoms of PTSD
- Exaggerated startle response, outbursts, physical and emotional reactions triggered by anything that resembles an element of the traumatising event. Marked avoidance of anything resembling the traumatic circumstances
- Nightmares, flashbacks, intrusive memories or visualisation of the trauma causing panic attacks/anxiety symptoms (sweating, palpitations, fight-or-flight response)
- Irritability, agitation, restlessness: sudden angry or violent outbursts. Muscle tension, some physical complaints
- Sleep disturbances - difficulty getting to sleep: early morning waking: circuitous thoughts preventing sleep: non-restorative sleep, leading to fatigue

- Hyper-vigilance, hyper-arousal, constant state of alertness to potential threat
- Memory and concentration problems
- Emotional numbing, sadness, depression, low self-esteem, guilt, shame. difficulty experiencing pleasure, loss of interest in activities formerly enjoyed, sexual dysfunction, phobic responses, feelings of mistrust, sense of detachment, hopelessness.

If you feel you may be experiencing post-traumatic stress disorder, please seriously consider getting expert medical or therapeutic assistance.

APPENDIX C

RECOMMENDATIONS FOR THE DESIGN OF SPACES THAT HOLD HUMANS

1   Windows that can be opened manually in addition to, or as an override of, electronically controlled windows, wherever possible: in cars, on trains, buses, taxis, coaches, in hospitals and other public buildings, hotels, shops, and so on

2   Doors that can be opened manually, wherever possible, in addition to, or as an override of, electronically controlled doors

3   Safety hammers to be fitted as standard in cars with laminated windows and central locking/anti-theft devices

4   Driving test to include questions on how to escape from cars in emergencies

5   Trains - a 'passenger communication protocol' for drivers, providing prompt information and regular updates when trains makes un-scheduled stops. Training for onboard staff on helping claustrophobic passengers

6   Lifts to be well-lit, fitted with long mirrors, and have clearly illuminated and well-maintained emergency instructions. Training for first response staff in premises with lifts on helping people with claustrophobia who become trapped

7   Attention to be paid to 'back of house' provision in hotels, department stores, hospitals, stations, offices and public buildings, to humanise the bleak, empty concrete stairwells and service areas often currently offered as alternatives to lifts or front-of-house facilities.

8   Loos - as per suggestions on p. 93. More 'community' provision in pubs and cafés, rather than electronically controlled street booths

9   MRI scanners - more 'open' and 'upright' facilities. In existing traditional facilities, more staff awareness about claustrophobia

10   Car-washes - clear information displayed outside facilities in which all four sides of the unit are closed during the wash programmes

11   Tourist attractions, 'stately homes', heritage sites - an open space/claustrophobia 'rating' giving advance warning of confined spaces that will be encountered on visits (such guidance is already supplied at the Pyramids, stating that visitors with back problems or who are prone to claustrophobia may experience difficulty since tours involve going through narrow, low ceilinged, unventilated passages)

12   Underground car-parks, subways, tunnels - clearer exit signs, consideration of stairwells as at 6, above, and more mirrors

This is a brief collation of ideas from the contributors.
If you have other suggestions you'd like to see highlighted,
please contact me via the publisher, at -
openspace@worthpublishing.demon.co.uk

Resources

BRIEF THERAPY/SOLUTION FOCUSED THERAPY

The Brief Therapy Practice in London pioneered the Solution Focused approach in the UK, and are leading providers of training and consultancy:
www.brieftherapy.org.uk
Lists of practitioner can also be found within the United Kingdom Association for Solution Focused Practice (UKASFP), www.ukasfp.co.uk

COGNITIVE BEHAVIOURAL THERAPY (CBT)

CBT is the therapy to which you are most likely to be referred through the NHS. However, if you want to find a private practitioner, contact:
The British Association for Behavioural and Cognitive Psychotherapies
BABCP, Victoria Buildings, 9 - 13 Silver Street, Bury, BL9 0EU Tel: 0161 797 4484
Email: babcp@babcp.com www.babcp.org.uk
or
The British Psychological Society (BPS) St. Andrew's House, 48 Princess Road East, Leicester LE1 7DR Tel: 0116 254 9568 Email: enquiry@bps.org.uk www.bps.org.uk

COMMISSION FOR ARCHITECTURE AND THE BUILT ENVIRONMENT

1 Kemble Street, London WC2B 4AN Tel: 020 707 6700 www. cabe.org. uk

COUNSELLING

The home for counselling in the UK is the British Association for Counselling and Psychotherapy (BACP). Through this organisation you can locate a counsellor from a wide variety of training disciplines.
British Association for Counselling & Psychotherapy
BACP House, 15 St. John's Business Park, Lutterworth, Leicestershire LE17 4HB
Tel: 0870 443 5252 www.bacp.co.uk

DUTCH SAFETY BOARD

Safety study on escaping from cars submerged in water (in English).
Also contains Instructions for Escaping from Vehicles (p.43 of the report), from the Dutch Institute for Road Safety Research (SWOV), and research findings indicating that many people's knowledge of what to do in the event of accidents, including which windows to break, could do with updating.
Visit www.safetyboard.nl/publications/dsb/safety_study_cars_submerged_in_water.pdf

EMOTIONAL FREEDOM TECHNIQUES (EFT)

To learn about EFT from the person who devised it, visit Gary Craig's website www.emofree.com To find a practitioner in the UK, www.eftmasters.co.uk

EYE MOVEMENT DESENSITIZATION AND REPROCESSING (EMDR)

The EMDR Europe Association has details of accredited practitioners available in the UK, through the NHS and privately. www.emdr-europe.org

FEARFIGHTER (Computer Assisted Cognitive Behaviour Therapy)

Quite a lot of information about what you might expect from this programme can be found at the *Fearfighter* website. To log on and use the interactive parts of the site, you will need an individual password, issued by the NHS.
Your first port of call can be your GP. www.fearfighter.com

FEAR OF FLYING COURSES

www.flyingwithoutfear.com   http://flyingwithoutfear.info/index.htm (Virgin)
www.aviatours.co.uk

INSPIRATIONAL POSTCARDS

Beautiful photocards of landscapes, plants, rocks and the ocean, linking gently positive messages to the natural world. A relaxing, sensory support for time spent in a confined space.
Self-esteem Building through the Creative Arts, at creativedrama@googlemail.com
Other peaceful imagery postcards can be found at www.worldspirit.org.uk

HELEN HAMLYN RESEARCH CENTRE

www.hhrc.rca.ac.uk

HYPNOTHERAPY

National Register of Hypnotherapists and Psychotherapists (NRHP)
NRHP, Suite B, 12 Cross Street, Nelson, BB9 7EN
Tel: 01282 716839 Email: admin@nrhp.co.uk www.nrhp.co.uk

KKE ARCHITECTS (Kirk Kavanagh Eguiguren Archichects LLP)

St George's House, 7-11 Lowesmoor, Worcester WR1 2RS
Tel: 01905 612863 www.kkearchitects.co.uk

LAUGHTER THERAPY

www.freewebs.com/laughtertherapy/researcharticles.htm for some fascinating ideas on the benefits of laughter (and some very bad jokes).

MRI

The first Upright MRI in the UK can be accessed privately or through NHS referral. The Upright MIR was specifically designed with claustrophobic patients in mind, and all staff are expert in patient care. Pictures of the scanner are on the website or on leaflets available from the Centre.
Upright MRI Centre, London, Julia House, 44 Newman Street, London W1T 1QD.
Tel: 020 7637 2888 www.uprightmri.co.uk
or

The Open MRI at the Nuffield Orthopaedic Centre NHS Trust (NOC) also takes referrals, and has photos of the scanner on their website. Staff are highly trained in supporting patients who experience claustrophobia.
Nuffield Orthopaedic Centre, Windmill Road, Headington, Oxford OX3 7LD
Tel: 01865 741155 www.noc.nhs.uk

NATIONAL PHOBICS SOCIETY

Established in 1970, this immensely helpful and supportive organisation has numerous resources and member services, including low-cost counselling and therapy and a newsletter. A user-led organisation, it is the largest UK charity dealing with anxiety disorders.
Zion Community Resource Centre, 339 Stretford Road, Hulme, Manchester, M15 4ZY
Tel: 0870 122 2325 Email: info@phobics-society.org.uk www.phobics-society.org.uk

NATIONAL INSTITUTE FOR HEALTH AND CLINICAL EXCELLENCE (NICE)

NICE is the body responsible for providing national guidance on the promotion of good health and the prevention and treatment of ill health. NICE recommends treatments for specific health problems. There is currently no specific recommendation for claustrophobia per se, but the recommendation for phobia in general currently favours CBT and computerised cognitive behaviour therapy The recommendations are updated regularly.
NICE - London Office, Midcity Place, 71 High Holborn, London WC1V 6NA
Tel: 020 7607 5800 Email: nice@nice.org.uk www.nice.org.uk

PSYCHOTHERAPY

The home of psychotherapy in the UK is the United Kingdom Council for Psychotherapy. Through this body you can find practitioners in Gestalt, Integrative, Narrative, Psychodynamic psychotherapy, and Transactional Analysis.
UKCP, 2nd Floor, Edward House, Wakely Street, London EC1 7LT
Tel: 020 7014 9955 www.psychotherapy.org.uk

RE-BIRTHING THERAPY

To find a practitioner in the UK, contact the British Re-birth Society
info@rebirthingbreathwork.co.uk Tel: 0845 3308214
www. rebirthingbreathwork.co.uk

SOLUTION FOCUSED – see Brief therapy, above

THOUGHT FIELD THERAPY

The British Thought Field Therapy Association's website gives information about TFT, a free download of the Thought Field Therapy Algorithm for the rapid treatment of traumatic stress, and a list of practitioners arranged by area and by training.
www.thoughtfieldtherapy.co.uk

WAYSFORWARD - SOLUTION-FOCUSED INTERACTIVE
COUNSELLING & COACHING SOFTWARE
A programme designed by experienced solution-focused therapists for adults
who want to think through problems and concerns, including claustrophobia. Can
be used individually or to support a helping relationship. Can be bought as an
individual CD Rom, installed for multiple users by an organisation, and from 2008,
will be available online at a low-cost pay-per-use.
Email: enquiries@waysforward.net www.waysforward.net

References

Accounts of people dealing with profound circumstances of being confined
Bettelheim, B. (1960) *The Informed Heart: a Study of the Psychological Consequences of Living Under Extreme Fear and Terror* London: Penguin

Johnston, A. (2007) *Kidnapped: and Other Dispatches* London: Profile Books

Keenan, B. (1993) *An Evil Cradling* London: Vintage

North, R. (2007) *Out of the Tunnel* London: Friday Books

Fear in context
Bourke, J. (2005) *Fear: A cultural history* London: Virago Press

Self-help books
Akers Douglas, A. (2006) *Flying? No Fear* Chichester, W. Sussex: Summersdale Publishers

Bloom, W. (2002) *Feeling Safe* London: Piatkus

Bourne, E. J. (2005) *The Anxiety & Phobia Workbook (4th Edn)* Oakland, California: New Harbinger

Butler, G. & Hope, T. (1995) *Manage Your Mind: the Mental Fitness Guide (2nd Edn)* Oxford: Oxford University Press

Dacey, J. S. & Fiore, L. B. (2002) *Your Anxious Child: How Parents and Teachers Can Relieve Anxiety in Children* San Fransisco, California: Jossey Bass

Edelstein, M. R. (1997) *Three Minute Therapy* Centennial, Colorado: Glenbridge Publishing

Flint, G. A. (2003) *Emotional Freedom: Techniques for dealing with emotional and physical distress* Veron, British Columbia: NeoSoTerric Enterprises

Godfrey, K. (2007) *Flying Without Fear* UK: Macroteach Publications

Griffin, J. & Tyrell, I. (2007) *How to Master Anxiety: All You Need to Know to Overcome Stress, Panic Attacks, Phobias, Trauma, Obsessions & More* Chalvington, E. Sussex: Human Givens Publishing

Hammond, C. (2006) *Emotional Rollercoaster: a Journey through the Science of Feelings* London: Harper Collins

Herbert, C. (2003) *Understanding Your Reactions to Trauma: a Guide for Survivors of Trauma & their Families (Revised Version)* Oxford: Blue Stallion Publications

Ingham, C. (2000) *Panic Attacks* London: HarperCollins

Kennerley, H. (1997) *Overcoming Anxiety: a self-help guide using Cognitive Behavioural Techniques* London: Constable & Robinson Ltd

Levine, B. E. (2001) *Commonsense Rebellion: Debunking Psychiatry, Confronting Society - An A to Z Guide to Rehumanizing our Lives* New York: Continuum

Levine, P. A. (2005) *Healing Trauma: A Pioneering Program for Restoring the Wisdom of Your Body* Boulder, Colorado: Sounds True Publishing

Matsakio, A. (2000) Emotional Claustrophobia: Getting over your Fear of Being Engulfed by People or Situations
Oakland, California: New Harbinger

Nelson-Jones, R. (2004) *Effective Thinking Skills* London: Sage Publications

Neuman, R. & Hanh, T. N. (2005) *Calming the Fearful Mind: A Zen Approach to Terrorism* Berkeley, California: Parallax Press

Perry, A. (2002) *Isn't It About Time? How to Stop Putting Things Off and Get On With Your Life* London: Worth Publishing

Perry, A. (2003) *The Little Book of Procrastination* London: Worth Publishing

Rowe, D. (2007) *Beyond Fear* London: HarperCollins

Sunderland, M. (2006) *What Every Parent Needs to Know* London: Dorling Kindersley

Thompson, G. (2006) *Fear: the Friend of Exceptional People* Chichester, W. Sussex: Summersdale Publishing

Counselling and psychotherapy

Bolton, G., Howlett, S., Lago, C. & Wright, J.K. (2004) *Writing Cures: An Introductory Handbook of Writing in Counselling and Therapy* Hove, E. Sussex: Routledge

Germer, C. K., Siegel, R. D. & Fulton, P. R. (2005) *Mindfulness and Psychotherapy* New York: Guilford Press

Gilbert, P. & Leahy, R. L. (2007) *The Therapeutic Relationship in the Cognitive Behavioural Psychotherapies* Hove, East Sussex: Routledge

Glicken, M. D. (2006) *Learning from Resilient People: Lessons we Can Apply to Counselling and Psychotherapy* Thousand Oaks, California: Sage Publications

Kinchin, D. (2007) *A Guide to Psychological Debriefing: Managing Emotional Decompression and Post-traumatic stress disorder* London: Jessica Kingsley

Macdonald, A. (2007) *Solution-Focused Therapy: Theory, Research & Practice* London: Sage Publications

Marks, I. M., Cavanagh, K. & Gega, L. (2007) *Hands-on Help: Computer-Aided Psychotherapy* Maudsley Monographs Hove, E. Sussex: Psychology Press

Shapiro, F. & Forrest, M.S. (1997) *Eye Movement Desensitization and Re-Processing: The Breakthrough 'Eye Movement' therapy for Overcoming Anxiety, Stress and Trauma* New York: Basic Books

Wells, A. (1997) *Cognitive Therapy of Anxiety Disorders: a Practice Manual & Conceptual Guide* Chichester, W. Sussex: Wiley

For children (but actually, quite helpful for adults as well)

Bombèr, L.M. (2007) *Inside I'm Hurting: Practical Strategies for Working with Children with Attachment Difficulties in Schools* London: Worth Publishing

Ironside, V. (2004) *The Huge Bag of Worries* London: Hodder
A funny and reassuring book, with lovely illustrations, about a little girl whose worries, stuffed into an increasingly heavy bag, are with her wherever she goes until she meets the old lady who knows what to do.

Sunderland, M. (2001) *Helping Children who are Anxious and Obsessional* – (includes story book, *Willy and the Wobbly House*, and guide) Bicester: Speechmark

Sunderland, M. (2003) *Helping Children with Fear* –(includes story book, *Teenie Weenie in a Too Big World*, and guide) Bicester: Speechmark
These two books form part of the excellent "Helping Troubled Children" series (Speechmark), designed to help parents and professionals help children with difficult and unmanageable feelings. The story can be used alone, or more powerfully, in conjunction with the guide, which explains the nature of the issues with which the child is struggling

Thomas, F. & Collins, R. (1999) *Supposing* London: Bloomsbury
This is a story about a little monster who becomes very anxious when his imagination runs riot. Supposing a disaster happened, and then a catastrophe, and then an even bigger nightmare? But mother monster is nearby to show how we can use "But supposing…?" to create soothing, pleasing images instead, as well as bigger, brighter, more exciting dreams (including toasted buns). Lovely book, perfectly paced, ideal for presenting our primitive brains with alternative, more helpful imagery.

ADDENDUM

In the course of my research, I was asked about implications for people in prison. As I've mentioned, the thought of being imprisoned, especially in over-crowded jails, is terrifying for people who hate and avoid confined spaces. Given the percentage of the population who feel this way, it reasonable to suppose there are many in prison who experience claustrophobia.

As this was my first book on the subject, I deliberately decided not to seek the experiences of prison inmates, as I felt my lack of knowledge might make such enquiry clumsy, possibly exacerbating an already difficult situation (of enforced confinement) for them.

I believe that as a society, we need to question whether the brutalising effect of struggling with anxiety and distress caused by being locked up for long periods, with uncertain access to visits, education, or mental health support, can really enable inmates to develop empathy for people they may have hurt, or the cognitive capacity to reflect on alternative ways of being and behaving.

John Samuels, QC, Chair of the Prisoners' Education Trust* wrote recently that if "*harsh conditions stopped people re-offending, prisons would not be overcrowded*", and that:

> "*Releasing an offender with nothing more than he went in - apart from a criminal record - will not help the offender, his family, or the society to which he returns*"
>
> (The Guardian, London, 15/11/07)

I hope an understanding of claustrophobia will contribute to the argument for prison reform.

---

* www. prisonerseducation.org.uk